CHILDREN
OF THE
POOR CLARES

CHILDREN OF THE POOR CLARES

The Story of an Irish Orphanage

Mavis Arnold • Heather Laskey

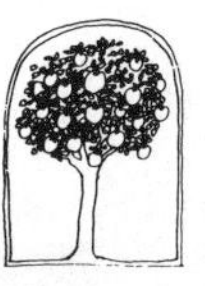

Appletree Press

for Anne, and for all the others

First published and printed by
Appletree Press Ltd
The Old Potato Station
14 Howard Street South
Belfast BT7 1AP
Tel: (0) 28 90 243074
Fax: (0) 28 90 246756
Web Site: www.appletree.ie
E-mail: reception@appletree.ie
1985

9 8 7 6 5 4 3 2 1

Acknowledgement is due to Dardis Clarke for permission to reproduce the poem by Austin Clarke on page 28.

British Library Cataloguing
in Publication Data
Arnold, Mavis
Children of the Poor Clares :
the story of an Irish orphanage
1. St. Joseph's Girls' Orphanage—Fire, 1943
I. Title
II. Laskey, Heather
363.3'79 HV887.I732C3
ISBN 0-86281-147-3

Contents

Acknowledgements 6
Prologue 7

Part One

1. Fire 15
2. Aftermath 24
3. Inquiry 30
4. Report 44

Part Two

5. 'One of the Good Schools' 51
6. 'A Greater Affliction' 61
7. 'A Substitute for the Family Life' 67
8. 'The Soil of the World' 82
9. 'God help the Poor Orphans, They're Not Normal' 89

Part Three

10. A Christian Country 123
11. Investigation 132
12. An Abdication of Responsibility 141

Epilogue 152
Notes 156

Acknowledgements

The authors would like to thank the following people for their help and advice in the writing of this book: Dr Timothy Brownlow, Mrs Constance O'Connell, the late Ian Harte, Yvonne Scannell and the women who told us their stories.

We are particularly grateful to the Department of Local Government and to the Department of Education whose officials worked so hard to make available to us the material relevant to the fire and especially the transcripts of the Tribunal of Inquiry.

We also thank our husbands, Bruce Arnold and Jim O'Brien, for their consistent support and encouragement through difficult times.

Note

The names of certain people mentioned in this book have been changed for the protection of the individuals concerned. The names of people quoted in published documents remain unchanged, as do those of people with public responsibility for aspects covered by the book.

It was the common practice of the girls in St Joseph's to address the Poor Clare nuns who looked after them as 'Mother', whereas they would normally be referred to as 'Sister'. Both forms of address are found in the book.

Prologue

Clare came to live with a family in a middle-class suburb of Dublin on a mild spring day in 1972. Tense, pale and unsmiling she carried a battered brown suitcase containing all her possessions. She was twenty-three years old, pregnant and unmarried. With no job, no money and nowhere to live she had gone to a voluntary agency, who had offered to find her a family with whom she could stay until her baby was born.

She was one of a large family. Her mother had disappeared when the youngest child was two, and the children were put into orphanages. Clare was four years old then and she and her three older sisters were sent to an industrial school – a state certified institution – in Cavan. She was to remain there for sixteen years and, after she left, had kept in touch with only one brother and one sister. She did not know what had happened to the others. She thought her mother was still alive.

She took time to become accustomed to her first experience of family life. Meal-times were the most difficult because she could not eat the food – saying it was too rich – and her fear of giving offence was so great that she would sometimes have to leave the table to go and be sick. At other times she would sit quietly, her shoulders hunched, rocking to and fro. She grew fond of the children, as they did of her, although she thought they needed much more discipline. She would look expectantly at their parents when she heard the children being rude, waiting for them to be beaten and surprised when they were not. She mistook the noisy games, the rivalry, the laughter, the tears for bad behaviour, unable to understand that it was the normal pattern of family life and that restraints could usually be imposed through love. Her own concept of discipline was very narrow and always based on physical punishment.

Obviously intelligent, she liked to help the children with their homework and was very shocked at how little Irish they knew. She was paid only a small amount of money in return for help in the house but she saved it carefully. She was clean, tidy and very reliable. She loved praise, although she found it hard to believe that she deserved it. If anyone was cross with her she would burst into tears and bite her nails furiously. She declared proudly that all the girls from the orphanage cried easily.

As the months passed she felt more at ease. Her suspicions and anxiety seemed to fade and to be replaced by trust. This, in due course, led to her confession a few weeks before her baby was due. Crying bitterly, she said this baby would not be her first. She had already had one other; it had been adopted.

After this, Clare talked more freely. She described her life in the orphanage, both pleased and surprised by the often horrified reaction to the stories of her childhood: the fear, the loneliness, the barely adequate diet and the endless beatings. She talked constantly about the other girls, some of whom she still saw and to whom her loyalty was intense. Many of them, like her, had moved from one domestic job to another, friendless and lonely, regarded as easy prey for any man who came along. They had illegitimate children and either had them adopted or else kept them, which resulted in a pitiful struggle to survive. Some of the girls married men who beat them, drank too much or deserted them. Others drifted into prostitution. A few, very few, had husbands who were 'good' to them. 'You feel ashamed to have been in an orphanage,' Clare would often say. 'You feel as if you belong nowhere. As if you're not good enough to be with ordinary people.'

Clare's daughter was born in the autumn. She decided to keep her although she was apprehensive about how she would manage, and when she left hospital both she and her baby were welcomed back into the family of which she had become inextricably a part. She had no difficulty in looking after the baby's physical needs: that came to her easily enough as she had looked after plenty of babies in the orphanage. But she had to be taught to show her affection: to hold the baby closely and to kiss and cuddle her. The family were sad when Clare made the sudden decision to leave them but she was determined to be independent. She got a job and put the baby into a day nursery. The next few years were difficult for her. Flats were expensive and she could only get low-paid part-time work. Her child was often sick and Clare spent many lonely days and nights looking after her. Her friends were girls in similar circumstances; penniless and alone.

All of Clare's brothers and sisters, with the exception of the youngest, a boy, were born during the 1940s. All of them spent the fifties in various institutions, four girls in one, two boys in another, three others (whose fates were never known to Clare) elsewhere. They were thus absorbed by the Irish industrial school system for upwards of two critical decades in their development, and emerged into a country substantially changed by social and economic progress. Though referred to as a false dawn, and with good reasons which were echoed elsewhere in the world, for Ireland the sixties were an outstanding period of optimism and development. Widening horizons of knowledge and awareness, steadily growing trade, highly successful tourism, the influence of television and the rapid growth of cultural activity was reflected in personal wealth and the rapid physical expansion of towns and cities.

Contraception was illegal and sex outside marriage was severely censored. Girls who had babies out of wedlock were condemned by their neighbours and often by their families. But for the affluent, the new standards, even in moral and religious terms, were easily acquired and readily modified. For the poor, the church remained powerful.[1] For the deprived, including Clare, its dominance was comprehensive and authoritarian. Such evidence of this 'good life' decade as impinged on her was malign. At the end of it she was to have the first of her two children out of wedlock. She had emerged from the protective isolation of an orphanage ill-equipped to cope with a changing world, and she suffered accordingly.

When Clare entered the orphange in which fourteen years of her life were to be spent, Ireland was an isolated and impoverished country. In addition to its geographic isolation, it was economically cut off from Britain by its own protective tariffs and from other European countries by the low levels of trading exchange. These were matched by social and cultural isolation in the days when tourism was a domestic pursuit at best, and there was no television to present a view of the outside world. The circulation of publications was modest, and severe censorship added a further barrier.

An even stronger emotional barrier derived from Ireland's wartime neutrality. The country had chosen this path under de Valera, to the dismay of the Anglo-Irish Protestants, to the satisfaction of active Republicans, and to the indifference of the majority, whose struggle for survival was substantially confined, by both tradition and the decision itself, to the twenty-six counties. Many men had emigrated to find work or to fight, and the resultant remittance mentality thus remained a central psychological force, though in practical terms emigrant labour contributed a flow of much needed revenue to depleted Irish families at home. But it did little to alleviate the 'lost world' feeling that prevailed during the post-war period of recovery and throughout the 1950s.

Not having been devastated by war Ireland was not orientated towards recovery in the same intense and determined way as the European countries directly affected by it. In the post-war years this resulted in a decline of confidence in the mid-fifties, so that by 1960, having gone through a relatively unstable succession of governments, alternating regularly between Fianna Fail and coalitions made up of various minority parties, the country was probably more backward, in relative terms, socially, economically and culturally, than any of its European neighbours.

This, briefly, is the background to Clare's infancy, childhood and adolescence. She had been sent to an orphanage in 1949 at the age of four. She did not emerge until 1966, shortly before it closed its doors. Though part of the industrial school system, St Joseph's, in Cavan town, with which her life became inextricably linked, was a rather special example.

* * * * *

> May 28th, 1861 – Three Sisters left our dear convent to found another St Clare's in Cavan for the education and salvation of the Little Ones of Our Divine Lord.
>
> *Annals of the Poor Clares*

Co. Cavan, an area of rocky hills, bogland and lakes was one of the poorer and more backward parts of Ireland. Its county town, of the same name, had a population of 3,400. It was set in a valley with old stone-built houses along the sides of the stream and rows of small brick terraced houses along the hillside. It had a typical wide eighteenth-century street and a courthouse and elegant Georgian houses lived in by the professional and well-to-do merchant classes and dominated by the new domed cathedral of the diocese of Kilmore. There was a slum, known as the Half Acre, where the poorest of the town lived, the old Market Yard, the town hall and a broad main street along which were located most of the shops and stores. This had been officially renamed Pearse Street in memory of the rebel poet and educational reformer executed in 1916.

Along this street for nearly eighty years had been the extensive premises of the Poor Clares. Behind the main buildings, their farm with a steward's house and farm buildings stretched up the hillside. There was an orchard and a well-tended vegetable garden. Below were the convent, a national school and the orphanage in whose walls, facing onto the main street, were barred opaque windows. The occupants of the convent were never seen outside, the orphanage children only rarely. Perhaps an older girl might be sent out on an errand or Maggie Smith might be seen walking slowly through the town. She had been in the orphanage many years before and had returned because she said that was where she wanted to die.

The Poor Clares were founded in Assisi, Italy in 1212. They were a contemplative order, but some of their members were engaged in the work of caring for destitute children and teaching. They were also famous for the lace-work and embroidered linen produced for sale in their convents.[2]

The industrial school system of which they were to become a part was introduced into Ireland in 1868 under the 1857 Westminster legislation. It followed hard on the heels of the reformatory schools legislation which was introduced to deal with young offenders. Although the purpose of industrial schools was to meet the needs of orphaned, destitute and abandoned children, they were always linked in the public mind with reformatories and criminal activity.[3]

When the legislation was introduced, the local authorities at the time were unwilling to contribute to the establishment of industrial schools or to the maintenance of the children. As a result various religious orders were requested to undertake the work. Where an Order was willing to do so, and where they could provide suitable premises, those premises were certified as fit for the reception of children in care. During the following years the number of certified schools increased until, in 1898, there were seventy-one of them caring for approximately 8,000 children. Five were for Protestants and fifty-six for Roman Catholics.

A weekly per capita grant of 5*s* was payable in respect of each child in care.

After Irish independence in 1921 the Department of Education took over the administration of all industrial schools. They came under the 1908 Childrens's Act which, with minor amendments, remains (in 1984) on the statute book. It laid down standards for clothing, food, education, training and discipline; it required that each industrial school should have a manager and be subject to annual government inspection.

By this time all these schools were for the reception of Roman Catholic children. One of the biggest, in Artane, outside Dublin, had 800 boys. Several of Clare's brothers were sent there. Children could be committed from the age of six to sixteen, after which they were under the manager's supervision until the age of eighteen, and only the Minister of Education was empowered to order a child's release.

St Joseph's Orphanage, Cavan, was certified as an industrial school for female children in 1869 and was to operate as such for close on 100 years. Though theoretically bound by certain rules and regulations it was to become a law unto itself. The Poor Clares were the only closed order to be given the care of children, and it was symbolic of the Roman Catholic Church's control over such institutions that a contemplative order of nuns, their lives shut off from the world, their concepts of love focused on Christ and Our Lady, should have been allowed by the state to have absolute charge of children deprived of normal family life.

The isolation of this small community behind its high walls in the centre of Cavan town was to have tragic consequences. On the night of 23 February 1943 fire broke out in the orphanage. For the first time in its history, the door of the Poor Clare convent were burst open by the outside world. Breaking locks and forcing doors, men intruded into the silent orderly life of the nuns. Within forty minutes the fire had taken the lives of thirty-five girls and the old woman, Maggie Smith, and, for a few weeks, was to bring St Joseph's and the town of Cavan into the public eye.

Part One

1

Fire

On the night of the fire, Tuesday 23 February 1943, a small group had gathered in the kitchen of Sullivan's, a general store whose premises were next door to the convent and overlooked the orphanage. Warmed by the new Aga stove, they were sitting up late over a game of penny poker. Members of the Sullivan family were there and also some of their shop staff, most of whom, as was the practice at that time, lived on the premises. Louis Blessing was visiting for the evening. A local Gaelic football hero, he was courting Cissie Reilly, the attractive girl who worked on the grocery counter.

Across the yard, in the orphanage, the electric lights had gone out at 8.30 p.m., and in the convent building by 10.30 p.m. The flicker of candlelight could be seen for an hour or so in two of the orphanage windows. The weather was fine and there was a light breeze blowing. Soon the street lights were turned off, and the last Garda foot patrol returned to the station. Over the road in Fegan's, the drapery shop, a foursome had returned at 1.30 a.m. from a badminton party. The two girls, sharing a bed in the room with their friends who lived-in, were giggling and gossiping into the night. At ten minutes to two, James Meehan, the town taxi driver, arrived at the Farnham Arms hotel to collect a passenger but found that the man had decided to stay the night.

At 2.0 a.m. the party at Sullivan's decided it was time for bed. Cissie Reilly looked out of the window into the yard to see what the weather was like. What she saw, billowing out of the vent in the orphanage, was smoke.

It was a few minutes later that Miss Bridget O'Reilly, asleep in her cubicle inside the Sacred Heart dormitory, was awoken by the sound of talking. Mary Caffrey, a sixteen-year-old girl, knocked at her door. Miss O'Reilly opened it – as she was to say later, 'a little bit' – and, on being told that there was smoke in the room, she instructed Mary and another girl to go to Sister Felix, one of the two nuns in charge of the eighty-two children in the orphanage, and, a few minutes later, she ran out of the room after the girls.

The buildings were in darkness, and to get to Sister Felix's cell the girls had to go down one flight of stairs to the first storey, through a corridor and up another flight of stairs. Mary tapped on Sister Felix's door, told her there was smoke in the dormitory and asked for the keys to the laundry, from where it seemed the smoke was coming. Sister Felix went into the convent, fetched some keys and gave them to Mary, who went off to the laundry. Meanwhile a few older girls left the dormitory to arouse others in St Clare's dormitory next door, and in Our Lady's dormitory downstairs. Miss O'Reilly arrived at Sister Felix's cell and, the Sister said later, asked that the electricity be turned on so that the source of the smoke could be identified. This was done by Sister Mary Clare, the other nun in charge of the children.

She had been woken in her cell in the convent and had come to Sister Felix's cell. When she turned on the main switch, it lit up the buildings, and simultaneously the electric bell on the main convent door began to ring. Sister Felix went to the Mother Abbess's cell where the front door key was kept. This she brought to Mary Caffrey who had returned from the laundry.

In the street a growing number of people had been shouting and pressing the doorbell in vain for five or six minutes. They hammered and kicked at the heavy door, and someone tried to batter it down with an axe. Cissie Reilly had woken up John McNally, another young live-in assistant at Sullivan's, and they had been joined by others, including the young men working at Fegan's, who had recently returned home from the badminton party. Louis Blessing had already run up the road to the Garda station to alert the police and had returned. James Meehan, the taxi driver, hearing the commotion, had driven down from the Farnham Arms, blown his car horn in an attempt to wake the nuns and then, urged by Blessing, had driven off to get the convent's farm steward, in the hope that he would have some way of entering the building. When they returned, the convent door was being opened by Mary Caffrey. They all rushed in and Mary showed some of the men to the laundry.

A scene of noise and confusion rapidly developed. With the exception of the steward, few of the rescuers had any knowledge of the layout of the buildings with their inter-connecting rooms, corridors and stairs.

But John McNally did know that the fire escape was located over the wooden landing from the top dormitories. As he ran through the door he saw a nun he recognised. 'Get the children out,' he shouted. 'Get everyone out! This fire looks to be dangerous.' She stood there and he implored her again, 'For God's sake, get them out or they will be trapped.' 'Try to put the fire out,' she said. 'But where is it?' he asked and she pointed to the laundry door and said something about keys. 'There's no time for keys,' he shouted and telling her to stand back, he booted the door open.

A couple of other men were beginning to go up the wooden stairs towards the dormitories without realising that this was the direct route up to the children, when a voice – which was never identified – from above called, 'Go back down.' Louis Blessing ran into the courtyard shouting, 'Where are the children?' and he and Cissie Reilly were directed by someone up the iron fire escape but, at the second floor, they were stopped by a locked door into a classroom. Blessing kicked at it, then tried to climb around it but failed, and they went down to find something with which to break it in.

After Miss Bridget O'Reilly had been to Sister Felix's cell, she went back up the wooden staircase to the top two dormitories and opened the door to St Clare's where, as she later put it, 'I was agreeably surprised to find that there was very little smoke. I then told everyone in the Sacred Heart, "You had better go into the other dormitory until we get the doors open and things fixed up."'

The sound of the girls running into St Clare's roused the children there. One girl remembers how, after she had been woken earlier, she got up, dressed and got back into bed with her head under the blankets, but her head 'went funny' and she got up again. 'By then the smoke was bad. That Miss O'Reilly saw me trying to get over to the window. "Get down on your knees and pray," she said. "Say an Act of Contrition." But I couldn't. I said I had to have air and crawled over to the window.'

The old woman, Maggie Smith, was seen coming in 'very pale-looking'. She walked over to an empty bed and lay down. No one saw her alive again.

Below, in Our Lady's dormitory on the first floor, the children had been woken and told by Miss Harrington, the other lay teacher, to go. They fled, coughing and crying down the stairs and out of the building.

Miss Harrington, having dressed, tried to go up the stairs but found them full of smoke. However, she told some of the older girls to 'run up to St Clare's and bring down the little ones.' Eighteen year-old Clare Shannon tried, but she could not get through the smoke. She then went out of the building, made her way round to the fire-escape stairs and tried to get up that way. She found that these, too, were impassable and met Louis Blessing, Cissie Reilly and a policeman as they came down.

These three had been up the outside fire escape a second time, bringing a mop to batter down the door at the top, but by then the smoke was very thick and when they got up to the top storey all the lights fused, plunging the building into total darkness. By the time they broke through into the classroom they could scarcely breathe. Just as they reached the external iron landing they saw the double fire-escape doors open, and Mary Caffrey came out, gasping for breath, followed by gushes of thick smoke. They could hear children crying and calling out that they were burning, but they did not know where to find them in the smoke and darkness. In fact, they were separated from the dormitory doors by only 7ft 6in of interior landing but they could only grope and choke their way back down.

At one point, a nun who was the convent bursar tried to get up the wooden stairs past Our Lady's dormitory, but was forced back by the smoke. She was about to attempt the iron staircase but hearing a knock at the hall door, went down to try to open it. Inadvertently she knocked down the bolt and called to the people outside they they should try the courtyard door. She said later that she then went to show some men where to get water and did not again attempt the iron stairs.

Another Sister tried without success to open the courtyard door to let people in, and then, going into the convent, found a man breaking the parlour window to get in that way. After Sister Felix had fetched the keys of the front door for Mary she had then gone through the corridor to Our Lady's dormitory to get the children out, but found nobody there. She said later, 'I went up no further because I think Mary Caffrey called to me for the keys of the new buildings.' On this bunch of keys was the one to the fire-escape doors. Sister Felix saw Sister Mary Clare, told her that Mary Caffrey wanted those keys and then, she claimed, tried to get up the iron fire-escape stairs, found the smoke very dark and was met by a man coming down who told her that she would need a gas mask to get up.

Sister Felix returned to the infirmary and helped some older girls to take the babies and little children who slept there to safety. Mary, having been given the keys by Sister Mary Clare, made her way up the wooden stairs. She was found outside Our Lady's dormitory by another girl, Una Smith, fumbling for the right key to the fire escape door. Soon she was feeling her way up the wooden staircase to the top storey. It was then that the lights fused, again plunging the building into total darkness. Mary unlocked the double fire-escape doors, and, gasping for air, called to the children to come out, saying that the doors were open. As she went out on to the iron landing she was seen by Blessing, Cissie Reilly and the gardai.

Una Smith, who slept in the Sacred Heart dormitory, had woken too late to hear Miss O'Reilly's order to go into St Clare's. After speaking to Mary, half way down the stairs, she realised that other children might be still asleep, so she went back up through the hot, dense smoke to the Sacred Heart. She felt all the six rows of beds and found one girl, Dolly Duffy, who was a bit deaf, still there. Una then got out through the now open doors to the fire escape, the only person, apart from Mary, to do so, while Dolly, after saying an Act of Contrition, put her apron over her head and went down the wooden stairs. She was the last person to escape this way. When she got out, the soles of her shoes were seen to be alight.

The dense smoke was now giving way to flames which, fanned by open doors, were spreading from the laundry wall timbers through the wooden stairs, the refectory, the kitchen and the classroom under St Clare's where over forty children were now trapped.

In the early minutes John McNally and his friend, John Paul Kennedy, one of the young men from Fegan's shop, had tried to attack what they thought to be the source of the fire – the laundry clothes drier – with fire extinguishers brought from the refectory by the nuns and Miss O'Reilly. When they were emptied, the men came out gasping for air. One of the nuns begged McNally 'like a good boy, try and go in again.' He asked for a wet cloth and Monaghan, the convent steward, tied it round his nose and mouth. Armed with fresh extinguishers brought from Sullivan's store, the two men went back into the laundry where, by this stage, the wooden walls were crackling with flames. McNally collapsed unconscious and was dragged by Kennedy out of the room into the courtyard. Kennedy then went up the wooden stairs as far as Our Lady's, but by then the stairs further up were already burning. When McNally recovered he was appalled to learn that, in spite of his entreaties to the nuns when he first came in, the children were still in the building. Directed by the convent steward who said to him, 'The kids are up there', McNally shouted for keys and tried to get up the iron stairs but the smoke was too thick.

Members of the town's fire brigade had, by then, arrived on the scene with a handcart and some lengths of hose in charge of the town waterworks caretaker. They had been brought to the fire by James Meehan, the taxi-driver. When the hose was connected to the standpipe out in the street, it was seen to be leaking so much that there was little pressure in the water coming out of the nozzle. It was useless.

Inside St Clare's, forty feet up from the ground, the older girls realised that they were trapped in the burning building. They made increasingly desperate attempts to get the younger children out of the door, but each time they opened it, the black smoke poured in. One of these girls was fifteen-year-old Kathleen Graham from the Sacred Heart. She had woken too late to hear the order by Miss O'Reilly to go into St Clare's but had gone there anyway to look for her seven-year-old sister, Bernadette. She could not find her.

When seventeen-year old Veronica MacManus looked down from a dormitory window into Sullivan's yard she could see flames coming from the classroom window below. In the yard people were shouting that ladders were coming, and she knocked on the window to attract their attention. Then she sat on a bed. Smaller children gathered round her and, coughing with the smoke, she began to lead them in a decade of the rosary: 'Hail Mary, full of Grace, the Lord is with thee. Blessed art thou among women and blessed is the fruit of thy womb, Jesus. Holy Mary, mother of God, pray for us sinners, now and at the hour of our death. Amen.'

Below, the yard was filling with people, clamour and turmoil. When the various attempts to reach the children from inside the building had failed, several of the men, including a policeman, had run through the unlit streets to the market yard where they knew the town council kept ladders, and tried to rouse the caretaker. There was no bell to his quarters, and after much yelling and shouting a window opened and, after a further delay, keys were thrown down only to be lost in the dark.

While this was going on, Louis Blessing had found a bicycle and pedalled furiously up to the Central Hotel where he and several other bachelors in the town had rooms, including Mattie Hand, who, as an electrician with the Electricity Supply Board (ESB), had a van with extending ladders. Blessing ran in shouting and roaring, and pulled Hand – who at first thought Blessing was joking – out of bed. While Hand dressed, Blessing cycled back to the market yard where he found people still stumbling around trying to find the ladders. He smashed open a door and, after more searching without light, they were located and a gang of men ran them over to Sullivan's yard.

Louis Blessing later described the scene there: 'The panic of the children seemed to be much worse then, and the whole place was pandemonium with the crowd and the children shouting, the glass and debris and pieces of slate and stuff coming down. . . the three windows were full of children. They seemed to have used every spot they could to sit on and hang on to.'

Kathleen Graham, who had gone into St Clare's to look for her younger sister, later told how it was during the saying of the rosary that the children began to scream. With another girl she went to the door to try to get out. When they opened it, they were overwhelmed by smoke. On the way back, the other girl, Mary Lowry, who wore a gold cross and chain around her neck, dropped to the floor, and Kathleen crawled under the beds to the window.

When Veronica was half-way through the third decade of the rosary, she could go no further. She and one of her closest friends, seventeen-year-old Ellen McHugh, looked out of the window and saw men putting up a ladder against the wall below and short of the window. 'Look,' cried Ellen, 'Oh, look! It doesn't even reach the window. How will we get down? Ellen and another older girl then made a last desperate effort to reach the door, but as soon as it was opened, flames poured in. Neither was seen again.

The rescuers had now been joined by a squad of soldiers stationed at a barracks in the town. They had been formed up on the parade ground and quick-marched in formation down the main street to the fire. Flames and smoke billowed out of the orphanage windows. The children were sobbing and screaming, calling out that they were burning, begging to be taken out. They saw the men struggling to extend the ladders. One went up partially but did not reach the window and came off the pulleys. The other had its ropes tied around it. The men got them untangled but still it would not extend. They lashed the two pieces together but as it went up they too swayed and fell apart, under the children's eyes.

At about this time the wooden staircase up to the dormitories collapsed. Louis Blessing later told how all he could see then 'framed against a background of flames was a sea of childish faces against the windows. I could hear them praying and coughing and calling, "Get us out, we are smothering." I think that the smaller ones who could not reach up to the window for air had no chance and must have been overcome at an early stage.'

The men were calling to the girls to jump from the window. The first to do so was Veronica. She was sitting on the window sill and when she saw flames coming from a cupboard at the far end of the dormitory, she just seemed to dive out of the window. Blankets were held out below but she crashed to the ground, breaking a hip and damaging an eye. A little girl jumped after her but she slipped through Blessing's outstretched arms and smashed her legs. Another fell on to a lean-to shed, bounced off it and hit the ground. After this, the other children were seen to draw back.

Miss Harrington, the teacher from Our Lady's dormitory, was standing near by. Earlier she had been calling up to the girls, 'Be quiet! ladders are coming.' She couldn't, she explained later, 'bring herself' to touch Maureen when she fell, but Dolly Duffy, the last girl to come down the stairs, took Maureen in her arms and carried the child to the hospital.

McNally, Meehan and a soldier then got a section of a council ladder and put it on the lean-to shed. McNally went up it and persuaded a girl to jump the gap into his arms. About three children got out this way, but when the last child jumped McNally lost his balance, he and the child fell on the shed roof and the ladder crashed to the ground. When McNally went up the ladder again and called, there was no reply from the window.

A survivor who was clinging on to another window sill later described the horrific scene inside the dormitory. 'The window was hot. The glass was cracking. The floor started to go – there were wardrobes and beds disappearing into the flames. I saw one girl lying unconscious on her bed, the clothes on her back on fire. Then she disappeared. Sisters were crying for each other with their arms outstretched. The two Cassidys were calling for each other. Then the floor where they were disappeared.'

When Mattie Hand, the ESB worker called by Louis Blessing, appeared his ladder was extended in seconds. He went up and began to bring down five screaming, choking, half-suffocated girls who were still clinging to the window sill. One of them – seven-year-old Bernadette Graham, whose sister Kathleen had earlier failed to find her – pulled back in terror into the room. There were only about eight feet of floor left. Theresa Brady, who was thirteen, went after her and, when Bernadette tried to wriggle out of her grasp, grabbed her by the hair, pulled her towards the window and took her down the ladders to Mattie Hand. Bernadette's back was badly burned, but she survived. Theresa was the last to come out alive.

Dr John Sullivan, brother of the Sullivans who owned the store, had the impression that there were still other children in the room, so he climbed up the ladder. 'When I got up abreast of the window, it was pouring smoke. The smoke got in my mouth and eyes and I had only time to try to have a look through and I got the impression that there was a heap or a pile of children about the level of the window. . . there were cries coming from it. . .

'It was pretty bad and I came down a step or two on the ladder to get air. I got under the sill of the window and stayed there for a couple of minutes to recover. During that period I could hear general crying or moaning coming from all over the room. I got up again to see if I could do anything, then I got a bit weak and I came down. I would have tried to get in if it were possible.'

As Dr Sullivan came down the ladder, flames burst through the windows of St Clare's dormitory. There was a terrible sound of crashing timbers. The time was approximately 2.40 a.m.

2

Aftermath

The flames were prevented from spreading into the convent building by the country's wartime Auxiliary Fire Service (AFS) trailer pump. It was not part of the town's fire brigade equipment, and was only brought to the fire because Louis Blessing sent James Meehan to arouse the crew. By the time a well-equipped fire brigade arrived from Dundalk, the nearest large town, it was 5.0 a.m. and the AFS had the fire under control. By daybreak only the burnt out shell of the orphanage remained, damp wisps of smoke curling up from the debris. The main convent building was out of danger and the Sisters were all safe.[1]

The children who had survived were scattered through the town. Some had gone to the house of a local physician, Dr Cullen. Others had fled in panic out into the fields behind the orphanage. People living on the outskirts of the town opened their doors in the early hours of the morning to find children sobbing out that the orphanage had been burnt to the ground. The babies and smaller children who had been taken from the infirmary were brought to the steward's house and, later in the morning, accommodation was found for all the children in the new sanatorium just outside the town.

One of the last children to escape alive had gone across to the hospital and sat with a girl who had jumped out of the window. 'Her teeth were all pushed in and she was spitting blood. Then a doctor came and I was frightened he would examine me so I ran out and went to Dr Cullen's house. The police were coming round to find out who had survived. Then I went over to the convent and went into the nuns and they sat up with me.'

The coming of daylight revealed to the people of Cavan the horrible extent of the disaster. All business premises were closed and in tense silence many people watched the removal of charred bodies from the heap of stones and burnt wood. There was a terrible stench over the town and the bodies, when found, appeared to the onlookers to resemble roast turkeys. The only body which could be positively identified was that of a seventeen-year-old who had round her neck a little gold cross and chain given to her by the previous bishop of the diocese as a prize.

One survivor recalled, 'In the morning I went through the yard. They were bringing out the bodies, sometimes just parts of bodies. A guard took me away from it and we were going out the courtyard door into the street when my sister came in. She looked at me as though she was going to faint. She said she had been going round and round and thought I must be one of the dead.' One man recalled for us his fruitless search from door to door for his two sisters, aged nine and sixteen, who had been put into the orphanage because of their mother's chronic mental illness.

The convent gardener was on his way to work when he met some of the local town councillors. His son recalls how, when they told his father about the fire, he first thought they were joking. 'He was a man who did not drink, but that night he went into a pub. He never really got over it. You see, he *knew* all those children.'

During the day, reporters arrived in the small town and watched with the local people while the thirty-six bodies were recovered and – never to be forgotten by anyone who witnessed it – placed in eight coffins. As the *Irish Times* reported it: 'Darkness was beginning to fall when the work. . . was completed. Many a strong man who wielded his shovel or pick with herculean energy during the day wept bitterly at the tragedy of the strange and silent coffining.' In a corner of the yard, three children were standing with the nuns and staring as the men shouldered the coffins, carried them to the convent chapel and laid them before the altar.

Dignitaries were arriving to express their condolences. The Bishop of Kilmore, Most Rev. Dr Lyons, visited the convent in the morning and spoke to an *Irish Times* reporter of the very fine work which the Poor Clares had done for a great many years in the town. Later, Mr Derrig, Minister for Education, arrived to sympathise with the Mother Abbess and the community. Callers at the bishop's house included Lord Farnham, the local big landowner, and Dr Lyons received many messages of sympathy from Cardinal MacRory and other members of the hierarchy, including Mr de Valera, the American ambassador, the British representative, the League of Prayer for the Canonisation of the

Blessed Oliver Plunkett and the Catholic Truth Society. During the days that followed, donations of several hundred pounds were to be given, as gestures of sympathy, to the Mother Abbess and to the bishop.

Irish newspapers gave wide coverage to the tragedy. In an interview, the Mother Abbess told a reporter that the children were never locked in their rooms at any time but could always gain access through the doors to the courtyard below. Her sister Miss Bridget O'Reilly, who had been in charge of the top two dormitories, said that the children received instruction in fire drill once a week and had been told to use the iron staircase in the event of an emergency.

The article continued: 'Police investigations have shown that none of the dormitory doors was locked but one door on the first landing of an iron staircase inside the building was locked. The children could have escaped by way of a corridor leading to another part of the building.' Another newspaper said that St Joseph's was considered to be one of the best industrial schools in the country.

Criticism about the inadequacy of the fire-fighting equipment was forcefully expressed in the press by some of those involved in the struggle to save the children. One anonymous trader was quoted as saying that 'the brigade was not fit to wash a bus', and Louis Blessing was reported in the *Irish Times* as saying that 'Cavan should be ashamed of itself. Had rescue apparatus been available in time, most of the children would have been saved.'

Two of the rescuers can never forget that terrible night. Mattie Hand, whose ESB ladder had enabled some children to be plucked from the edge of the inferno, said, 'The place went up like a box of matches because of all the polishing they had to do. It was Lent at the time and we were all on the tack, but we had to go on the beer after that. The *Irish Times* were after me, buying me beer, trying to get a criticism of the nuns from me. I drank their beer but said nothing.'

John McNally said, 'That night changed me. I was divil-may-care before. I'd go to the pictures and dances with lots of fellows and girls, but after seeing the children and old Maggie Smith. . . only a couple of days before I'd repaired a religious statue for her. It had belonged to her mother and I suppose it was burned along with her. After the fire I started to realise what it was to be still alive. It made me kinder. At first I couldn't sleep, nor could a lot of us. I could still see and hear the children for a long time.'

An inquest on the victims was opened and adjourned *sine die* at the Cavan courthouse. Mr P. N. Smith, solicitor and town councillor, who appeared for the community of the Poor Clares, said that every help would be given by the Sisters to the investigation of all circumstances of the tragedy.

The funeral took place on Thursday 25 February. Requiem mass was celebrated in the convent chapel by the bishop, while the nuns stood silently behind their grille at the back of the church. At the end of the mass the coffins were carried through the convent grounds by members of the local security force past the still-smouldering ruins of the orphanage. Lying against the wall in the yard was a pile of hoops which the children had played with the day before they died. As the nuns passed the burnt-out buildings, they were seen to weep. They left the cortège when they reached the convent gates.

A crowd of several thousand people had gathered silently in the main street to watch as the coffins were put into hearses, and the funeral procession began its journey to Cullies Cemetery outside the town. There, as a reporter described it: 'Men and women broke down and wept as the eight nameless coffins containing the remains of the thirty-five children were lowered into the huge grave. The most tragic figures in the crowd of mourners were two fathers and a mother, each of whom had lost two daughters.'

At mass in the cathedral on the following Sunday the bishop asked the congregation 'to pray for comfort to be given to the relatives and friends of these little angels and to the dear Sisters who have devoted themselves to the care of these children for the love of God, so tenderly and successfully. . . you can realise what a terrible ordeal it has been for the good nuns to have the fierce glare of publicity turned on their quiet sheltered lives while weeping over the loss of these little ones. St Joseph's Orphanage is an institution of which Kilmore diocese has reason to be proud. I exhort the faithful to pray fervently and humbly that it may please Almighty God to accept the sacrifice of these little ones, and thus ward off a greater affliction.'

Later in the week, after some repairs to damaged parts of the convent building, the remaining children were brought back in motor cars from the sanatorium. 'Before leaving,' the local newspaper, the *Anglo-Celt*, reported, 'they thanked the ladies of the Red Cross, the country and town Medical Officers of Health for their kindness and those of the children spoken to expressed their pleasure at returning to the nuns in the convent.'

At a meeting the following Monday, the Urban District Council (UDC) discussed allegations in the national newspapers about the lack of fire-fighting equipment. A councillor complained that Cavan had been disgraced in the *Irish Times* (at that time, a predominantly Protestant and Unionist newspaper). Mr Gaffney, the town surveyor, said there was no doubt that there was sufficient equipment at the fire to deal with it – 'As far as we are concerned everything was in perfect order.' He was supported by the other councillors except for one who, when he enquired what the arrangements were for calling out the brigade, was asked by the chairman, Miss Brady, 'Are you criticising the council?'

During his funeral oration in the convent chapel, the eight coffins laid out before him, the Bishop of Kilmore had said, 'In the presence of this terrible calamity, which it has moved Almighty God to visit on us, we bow our heads in resignation and humility. . . . These little children, who had not the care of their parents, but had a beautiful substitute in the gentle protection of the Sisters, were snatched away in the dawn of life. Dear little angels, now before God in Heaven, they were taken away before the gold of their innocence had been tarnished by the soil of the world.'

His words were to be used later by the poet Austin Clarke:

Martyr and heretic
Have been the shrieking wick.
But smoke of faith on fire
Can hide us from enquiry
And trust in Providence
Rid us of vain expense.
So why should pity uncage
A burning orphanage,
Bar flight to little souls
That set no churchbell tolling?
Cast-iron step and rail
Could but prolong the wailing:
Has not a Bishop declared
That flame-wrapped babes are spared

Our life-time of temptation?
Leap, mind, in consolation
For heart can only lodge
Itself, plucked out by logic.
Those children, charred in Cavan,
Passed straight through Hell to Heaven.

3

Inquiry

One week after the fire, Mr Sean MacEntee, Minister for Local Government and Public Health, whose department was responsible for fire brigade organisation, moved a motion in the Dáil to set up a Tribunal of Inquiry. 'It is expedient that a Tribunal be established for inquiring into the following matters of urgent public importance, that is to say: the cause of the fire which occurred during the night of Tuesday 23 February 1943 at St Joseph's Orphanage, Main Street, Cavan, and the circumstances in which loss of life was occasioned by the said fire, and to make such recommendations in relation thereto as the tribunal may think proper.'

During the debate on the motion a week later in the Seanad, the Senator from Cavan, Patrick Baxter, was at pains to defend the town and to refute press criticisms, especially those in the *Irish Times* of its fire-fighting facilities. He also said there had been 'statements about the difficulty of gaining access to the building and about the difficulty of procuring keys. All these had been a misrepresentation of the facts.' Mr MacEntee, a senior member of Eamon de Valera's government, repeating a point he had made earlier in the Dáil, replied that the purpose of the commission 'was not so much to find scapegoats as to try and find what were the weaknesses which led to the loss of life and devising preventitive measures. . . . It might convey a wrong impression of my point of view if it were assumed that the commission would not have to fix responsibility.'

The members of the Tribunal of Inquiry were: Mr Joseph McCarthy, Senior Counsel (Chairman), Major James Comerford, Chief Superintendent of the Dublin Fire Brigade and Mrs Mary Hackett, who was described in newspaper reports as being well-known in connection with social services in Dublin. The secretary of the tribunal was Mr Brian O Nualláin, an official from Mr MacEntee's department.

The tribunal began its sittings in the Cavan courthouse on 7 April.

The hearings lasted for eleven days during which sixty-four witnesses gave evidence: thirteen girls from the orphanage, eleven nuns, two lay teachers, several of the people involved in the rescue attempts, local authority employees, experts in different fields and two industrial school inspectors.

A tribunal of inquiry is not a court of law, and members of a tribunal are not judges. The role of counsel and solicitors is to represent groups or persons whose interests are threatened or who need to be protected.

The interests at stake here were the Cavan Urban District Council, which had responsibility for local fire-fighting; the Department of Education, which had statutory responsibility for the administration of Industrial Schools; the Electricity Supply Board, represented because it had been suggested that the fire was caused by an electrical fault; the Order of Poor Clares and their employees, and the girls from St Joseph's Orphanage. Counsel were briefed to represent the UDC, the Department of Education, the ESB, the Poor Clares and their employees. The General Solicitor for the Wards of Court was represented by a solicitor, as were three next-of-kin.[2]

The responsibility for providing fire-fighting arrangements lay with the UDC, although at this time they were under no statutory obligation to do so. The thrust of their argument was that any shortcomings in their fire-fighting arrangements were not responsible for the loss of life. The case made by their counsel was that there was no proper turn-out of the town fire brigade on the night of the disaster because the captain had not been called, and that the council's equipment – a hose on a handcart, and two extending ladders – were in good working order.

Mr P. Gaffney, the town surveyor, said that he inspected the brigade's equipment at least once a week, and that it was 'in perfect order'. He admitted, however, that the UDC ladders were not part of the equipment and that the lack of arrangements for rescue work was 'because no case requiring ladders had ever arisen' and, anyway, that the 'whereabouts of the ladders was generally known on the night of the fire'.

The failure of the council's ladders was considered by many to have been a contributing factor in the deaths of the children. It had taken a long time to locate the ladders and bring them to the fire. They did not extend properly, did not reach windows and fell apart. The council employee responsible for their care and maintenance was Mr Thomas Smith, weighmaster for the previous thirty years. He told the inquiry that he lived in the market yard building where 'potatoes, oats, hay and such' were kept. His job was to 'weigh stuff', keep the place clean, caretake and hire out the extending ladders. These, he insisted, were not for fire-fighting though he claimed they were always returned to the market yard at night.

He said that to get the ladders at night it would be necessary to rouse him, or rather his wife. 'I sleep in the back and the woman sleeps at the front' – a piece of information which, together with his habit of speaking through his moustaches, produced guffaws in court. To wake her it would be necessary to shout because there was no bell or knocker. To the chairman's question, 'Did you ever think that the ladders might be wanted for a fire?' Smith replied, 'Well, you cannot foretell.' He insisted that the ladders were in perfect order before the fire.

During the evidence of three men – Louis Blessing, John McNally and John Kennedy – who had played brave and active parts in the rescue attempt, the UDC counsel tried to prove that they did not know how to use the ladders and extended them wrongly. Both McNally and Kennedy insisted that the ladders had been pulled correctly as they used to demonstrate them in the course of their work in hardware shops, but that the ropes were off their pulleys. The chairman was overheard saying to counsel in respect of McNally, 'You are wasting your time. That man seems to know what he is talking about.'

The town's only official fire-fighting equipment was a hand cart and some lengths of hose. When the hose was connected up to the street hydrant soon after 2.20 a.m. it was seen to be leaking in several places. The equipment was in the charge of Mr James Fitzpatrick, the town's waterworks caretaker, and he was responsible for its maintenance. He told the tribunal that he had twenty-two years experience with fires and the hoses were in 'splendid condition'. 'After a fire is over I take the hoses down and wash them and I test every length by itself and put it out to dry.' Then he would leave it on the hand-cart.

He was brought to the fire by James Meehan, the taxi-driver. He said that he supervised the hose which, on the advice of the convent steward, he played into the refectory 'to keep the fire from getting into the main building.' During his evidence he used phrases like, 'I went out to see what was proceeding there' and 'there was smoke and a nice blaze coming out.' He agreed that there had been a lot of talk about the fire in the town but said he did not join in – 'I have enough to do to mind the water' – and added that because he, Fitzpatrick, had been called, Meehan could be thanked for the convent not being burned down.

The history of the fire brigade itself appeared somewhat obscure. In 1940 Mr Gaffney was given responsibility for it, but the man who was in charge of the AFS told the tribunal that it was impossible to get crew because 'the apathy was terrific and they kept falling away.' There was uncertainty about who constituted the brigade. James Fitzpatrick, for example, maintained that although he 'turned out' with the brigade he was not actually in it. When the chairman enquired whether he got anything extra for this, Fitzpatrick growled, 'All I ever got for any fire work I did was plenty of abuse', at which there was laughter in court.

Several members of the brigade described the call-out procedure. One man told the inquiry that he knew of no call-out instructions except that Fitzpatrick was to call him. Another said that their training was 'all perfunctory', they had no practice with a ladder, only with 'putting water on.' Patrick Cullen, the captain of the brigade said that he had been chosen as captain because he lived at the town hall, and that was where the Brigade assembled. He was not 'really' but only 'sort-of' captain. At fire drill he never took charge or gave instruction. He described the call-out routine. He was to be called first, and then the rest were to be called in turn, each one bicycling off to get the next.

Major Comerford: 'Was there any means of calling you at night?'
Cullen: 'Not unless they kicked the door.'
Comerford: 'No bell or knocker?'
Cullen: 'No.'
Comerford: 'How long would it take to assemble everyone at the town hall?'
Cullen: 'Judging from previous occasions I would estimate about three-quarters of an hour.'

(This was the same period of time as had elapsed between the smoke first being seen from Sullivan's, and the final collapse of the dormitory floor.)

Chairman: 'Was this little fire drill you had just an afternoon's amusement?'

Cullen: 'No, it was in case of emergency.'

Because St Joseph's was a certified industrial school, most of the children had been admitted to it through the courts by the Department of Education. The Department's duty was to ensure that the children were adequately protected by the relevant legislation and that the regulations were being implemented. Yet in the statement with which he opened the inquiry, Counsel for the Department, Mr McLoughlin, clearly defined his role as one of only 'assisting' the inquiry.

'The orphanage,' he said in his opening statement, 'being a certified school, is subject to inspection by the Minister. This school has been regularly inspected and would appear to have carried out its duties to the children in all particulars. Following the receipt of circulars from the Department of Education about regular fire drill, the Department had been informed by the Manager in a letter that it had been put into effect.'

(Fire Drill was required by the regulations to take place once every three months, each alternate drill at night, and a record had to be kept in the school diary.)

Mr McLoughlin called Dr Anna McCabe, Medical Inspector of Industrial and Reformatory Schools, who testified that, during her visits to the orphanage, she had been satisfied that all the regulations, including compulsory fire drill, were being carried out to her satisfaction. The children's legal status was then clarified by Mr Roe, Counsel for the Order.

Mr Roe: 'This is an Industrial School and the children have to be detained in it. They are not permitted to go out?'

Dr McCabe: 'Yes. . . it was a very well managed school.'

Mr Roe: 'In a school of this kind where the children are in a sense prisoners, what are the relations between the children and the nuns?'

Dr McCabe: 'Excellent. In fact this is one of the good schools. . . although this is an enclosed order, they do not suffer any restraint. They were intelligent and active children. They were allowed out and about. They had every facility. They were all normal children.'

Although fire escapes were not compulsory in any state institution at that time the Cavan orphanage did have one, but during the fire only

two girls out of the eighty-two in the building actually escaped that way, in spite of the fact that the double fire escape doors leading indirectly – through the classroom – on to it was only seven-and-a-half feet away from St Clare's dormitory. Criticisms about its location had been made in the *Irish Times,* and this may have been one of the reasons why Mr McLoughlin called the architect who had drawn up the plans for the fire escape to give evidence. When questioned, he admitted that the location of the fire escape would not have been up to standard regulations. 'Being an industrial school you don't want to have a stairway where people would have access to it other than the people in the institution and you are not always free to put it where you like.'

In his opening statement, Mr McLoughlin said that he would make no conjecture as to the cause of the fire, but then contradicted this by saying, 'There would be evidence that there was something wrong with the lighting arrangements in the orphange previous to the fire, and that it was because of this that the main switch in the convent and orphanage premises had been turned off on the night of the fire.' In fact the electrical system was found, on technical grounds, not to have contributed to the disaster in any way. Furthermore, according to a nun's evidence later, the turning off of the main switch was a routine procedure.

Mr McLoughlin then added, 'Cavan Urban Council were not to blame because the modern fire equipment ordered from Britain had been refused. . . . There had been a confused account of what happened inside the orphanage, but one thing is clear, that from the time the alarm was given until assistance arrived nothing more could have been done and no more children could have been rescued in the circumstances.'

This was later to be contradicted in the tribunal's report where it was estimated that, in the first fifteen minutes after the discovery of the fire, the children could have been taken out safely. They also concluded that the building had not been adequately inspected as a fire hazard, and that the Department had not acted in a satisfactory manner in this regard. They did not comment on the unsuitable location of the fire escape, nor on the fact that the children's status as *de facto* prisoners – a situation for which the State and not the Order was ultimately responsible – was in any way a contributory factor to their deaths.

The evidence of the nuns – eight of whom were called – was heard in the convent parlour. As an enclosed order, they were not allowed to leave the confines of St Joseph's. They were treated with courtesy and consideration, and the tribunal expressed its sympathy to them for the disaster.

The Mother Abbess was, according to industrial school regulations, the manager of the school, the legal guardian of the children and, thus, the person with the ultimate responsibility for them. In spite of the fact that she was roused early during the fire for the front door keys, kept in her cell, she made only one statement to the inquiry. Asked if she was manager of the school she replied that she was, but that she had appointed Sister Mary Clare to look after the work for her. She was asked no further questions.

The first concern of the nuns, immediately after they were roused on the night of the fire, had been the fetching and giving out of keys. Some handed out fire extinguishers, showed where water was to be found, tried to open doors to the street and, aided by older girls, brought the babies from the infirmary, in the relatively unaffected wing of the orphanage, to safety.

In their evidence they described their evening duties, in particular which doors were locked by whom and where the keys were kept. One nun told how she had charge of the keys after the portress locked the street doors and would then take them to the Mother Abbess. A teaching nun said she locked the doors after classes 'including the emergency door from St Clare's and the Sacred Heart on to the iron staircase and the door that leads from the classroom to the iron stairs. I hang the keys on the nail outside the Mother Abbess's door.'

Another teaching nun, who had said the rosary with the children on the night of the fire, stated that 'All the dormitory doors were unlocked. . . all I would do at night was to turn off the light and lock the classroom doors out to the iron staircase.' Several of the Sisters, according to their evidence, tried to go up the wooden stairs but they never got past Our Lady's dormitory on the first floor. Sister Mary Clare, to whom had been delegated the role of acting manager of the orphanage , told how, after she had given Mary Caffrey a bunch of keys – including the one to the emergency door – she then went and dressed.[3] After that she showed the rescuers where the fire extinguishers were kept and made her way down the iron staircase. She said she

heard Sister Mary Felix calling out that it was smokey and then met two men coming down who said, 'They are not there. Go back. They are being got out into Sullivan's yard.' And so she went down.

Sister Felix told the inquiry that, after she had got the front door keys from the Mother Abbess and given them to Mary Caffrey, she later went up the wooden stairs to Our Lady's Dormitory 'to get the children out quickly, but I saw nobody there.' Asked if she went up further she replied, 'No, I think Mary Caffrey called to me for the keys of the new building.' Having got these keys for Mary, she said she then tried to go up the fire escape 'but the smoke was very dark' and, she added, 'a man told me we could go up if we had gas masks.'

Several attempts were made during the course of the inquiry to get corroboration of this meeting from the outside rescuers, particularly from Louis Blessing, but none could recall it despite repeated questioning. However, in their report, the tribunal stated, 'In view of the fact that they did go directly to Sullivan's yard, we accept the Sisters' recollection on this point.'

The issue of fire drill was clearly of importance. Mr McLoughlin had earlier called both a Senior Inspector and Dr McCabe from the Department of Education to confirm that it had been carried out according to the regulations.

During her evidence, Sister Mary Clare explained the routine: 'The children were told that if fire was anywhere in the basement they were to go out on the iron staircase, and if it was somewhere in the convent they were to go down the wooden staircase towards the laundry.' She admitted that fire drill had never been held in the dark. She said she would ring a handbell and call, 'Fire, rise, bathroom lobby exit. . . and then they marched out. The children did it very well.' She added that Miss O'Reilly never took part in the instructions. 'She knew nothing of the drill. The children knew.' She explained that the emergency door on to the fire escape was locked but that it was a double door of the kind that could be opened directly by pulling down the bolts from the inside. She said that most of the older girls knew how to do this. 'The pupils often opened the door at night to chase pigeons.'

The evidence of the nuns was accepted largely without comment. Sister Mary Clare was never asked the most important question of all – why the routine, practised four times a year according to the diary, and understood by the children, had not been followed on the night of the disaster. The children, however, were to be asked this question repeatedly when their turn came to give evidence.

For the moment, Mr Roe, Counsel for the Order, summed up what he considered to be the essence of the case. 'At the time of the fire the nuns were unfortunate in getting an unfavourable press and in a number of stories which were circulated. There was some prejudice against the Order because it was enclosed. There was a great deal of talk as to whether such an Order was the proper one to have charge of an institution of that kind. The tribunal has seen the convent and the girls and the greatest testimony to the nuns was the affection between them and the girls. . . . The nuns had also been subjected to a great deal of criticism in respect of things that had not happened at all.

'There was a suggestion that the orphans had all been locked in their dormitories as if they were in prison cells and could not escape. That was untrue and again it was also untrue that the nuns had refused to open the door and admit people to help them and that some of the children had fled from the town and taken refuge in farmers' houses. . .[4]

'The way my clients view the inquiry is that their function was not to find a scapegoat but to make recommendations towards saving life in similar circumstances in the future. I hope that in your report no blame whatever would be attached to the nuns and I submit that there was no blame to be cast upon them.'

Miss Bridget O'Reilly, lay teacher and sister of the Mother Abbess, was then called to give evidence. It was she who went down to Sister Mary Felix's cell, returned, ordered the children from the Sacred Heart into St Clare's dormitory, and then went down the wooden stairs to safety. In her evidence she disclaimed any responsibility for the children in the dormitories, insisting that she was not 'in charge', but only there 'to keep order and give out aspirins'. She maintained that she could not at any stage have brought the children down the stairs. She knew the door to the fire escape was locked but did not know it could be opened without a key. She said she had never taken part in fire drill, though she thought the fire escape door was the right way out during a fire.

She said that, when she went down the stairs for the second time, having told the girls in the Sacred Heart to go into St Clare's 'until we get the doors open and things fixed up' that she gave a man some fire extinguishers hanging on a wall in the refectory. Then, 'I got a shock because the smoke was on the stairs. . . something snapped in my head and I could not remember where I was then.' When pressed for an explanation of her conduct, she said, 'I don't know', or, 'My mind is gone odd', or, 'My memory is gone in parts.'

She was later recalled by the chairman and asked her age. The chairman suggested fifty but she replied that she was forty-six. She said she could not remember how long she had been in the orphanage but that it was about ten years. Before that she had taught in another industrial school.

Chairman: 'It may be an excusable error on your part, but, looking back on it, hadn't you a good reason for going back and getting those children out?'

Miss O'Reilly: 'I don't exactly know.'

Chairman: 'Were you not worried about them when you went downstairs for the second time?'

Miss O'Reilly: 'I was quite happy about them being out of the smoke in St Clare's.'

In effect the children had no legal representation. A lawyer did represent the General Solicitor for the Wards of Court, but he played no part in the proceedings. Neither did the solicitors representing the next-of-kin of six dead children. The thirteen girls called by Mr Roe, Counsel for the Order, appeared on behalf of the nuns, in whose care they and their dead friends had been.

The inquiry took place less than two months after the fire. Two of the girls called to give evidence had been injured. Another fainted the first time she was put on the witness stand, but was brought back the next day. Each girl gave her age and, if over fifteen, her occupation in the orphanage: portress, cook, laundress, maid or needleworker.

The question of fire drill arose almost immediately. One fifteen-year-old was asked by Mr O'Higgins, Counsel for the ESB, 'When you left the dormitory you did not go out to the emergency door?'

No reply.

Chairman: 'You have done fire drill?'

Answer: 'Yes, sir.'
Chairman: 'Did you know from the fire drill the way to go out on to the iron staircase?'
Answer: 'Yes.'
Chairman: 'Why didn't you go out on to it?'
Answer: 'I did not think of going that way.'

Pressed further on this point 'No reply' is recorded several times.

Questioned by Mr Roe, another fifteen-year-old girl agreed that she had done fire drill. She said she did not think of using it that night and she did not know that the fire escape door could be opened without a key. A sixteen-year-old said she had been in St Clare's dormitory for over a year but, during that time, she had not taken part in fire drill.

Mr McLoughlin: 'Did Sister Mary take you for fire drill?'
Answer: 'No.'
Mr McLoughlin: 'Who did?'
The chairman intervened: 'Who gave the fire drill in St Clares's for the past twelve months?'
Answer: 'Sister Mary Clare.'
Mr McLoughlin: 'Did you know how to get out on the fire escape?'
Answer: 'Yes, I had been out there to chase pigeons.'

The most important door for the purposes of the inquiry was the fire escape door, close to St Clare's dormitory over a wooden landing. That was why the nocturnal pigeon-chasing was so important. Yet, all those girls who walked out of the building did so down the wooden stairs until Mary Caffrey unlocked the fire escape door with a key. But this, according to Sister Mary Clare, could have been done without a key. Why, then, was Mary given one? The question must have arisen in other minds too. The day after Mary had given her evidence, Mr Roe made a statement: 'To avoid embarrassment we must point out that Mary Caffrey is not and never has been a pupil at the industrial school.' The embarrassment, as he implied it, was of a social nature. The point, however, was that non-pupils, according to the regulations, were not required to take part in fire drill. Thus, she would not have had to know how to open the door without a key.

Veronica MacManus, a laundry-worker, aged seventeen, who had nearly died from her injuries when she jumped out of the window, had been in charge of St Clare's dormitory. She was asked a total of five hundred questions, far more than anybody else at the inquiry. At one point the chairman repeatedly asked her how the children in the dormitory were behaving, and then the questioning was taken up by Mr Roe.

Mr Roe: 'Did you hear anybody calling out to come down by the stairs?'
Veronica: 'Yes, I can remember someone shouting, "Come down by these stairs and you will be safe".'
Mr Roe: 'Why didn't you go out then?'
Veronica: 'I could not move. I was so weak.'
Mr Roe: 'You said there that you were weak and that is why you did not go out, but after that you kicked out the window, didn't you?'
Veronica: 'Yes.'
Mr Roe: 'When you heard that voice did you say anything to any of the children?'
Veronica: 'No, I could not speak at all at the time.'
Comerford: 'After the call at the landing were the children shouting?'
Veronica: 'They had ceased shouting at that time.'
Chairman: 'When do you remember first hearing the children shouting?'
Veronica: 'I think it was while we were saying the second decade of the rosary.'
Comerford: 'How long after that did you notice anything wrong with any of the children?'
Veronica: 'About ten minutes after that.'
Comerford: 'When first did you feel frightened?'
Veronica: 'When I first went over to sit on the window.'
Comerford: 'Did you remain frightened all the time?'
Veronica: 'I just felt I was going to die at that minute, sir.'

Veronica was cross-questioned by all the members of the tribunal including Mrs Hackett, who said virtually nothing else, and by nearly all the counsel.

Polly Doyle, aged sixteen, was also asked similar and numerous questions.

Chairman: 'When was it that the children started shouting?'
Polly: 'The shouting started when the smoke came in.'

Chairman: 'When did the shouting stop?'
Polly: 'When I was out on the window-sill all the blazes were in the dormitory. It was then they gave up shouting.'
Chairman: 'Did you see the fire getting near any of the children?'
Polly: 'I saw it coming up nearer every time, sir.'
Chairman: 'Did you see anybody that the flames got near?'
Polly: 'I could not say really.'
Chairman: 'But was the fire actually getting near all the children?'
Polly: 'I do not know that.'
He persisted with this question.
Polly: 'I could see all the flames, but I did not see any children.'
Chairman: 'Did the children at any time go to the end corner of the dormitory and try to huddle together in any way?'
Polly: 'I do not know. . . .'
Chairman: 'Were you excited? Did you get hysterical?'
Polly: 'Yes.'
Chairman: 'You know what I mean – were you shouting and shrieking?'
Polly: 'Yes.'
Chairman: 'Were you afraid that you would be burnt alive?'
Polly: 'Yes.'
Mr McLoughlin: 'It is fair to say that this girl's recollection of events is not too sound. She has done her best of course.'

Theresa Brady, aged thirteen, was repeatedly questioned both by Mr Roe and the chairman, who asked her about the actions of the older girls who had died. Finally she said, 'Please, sir, I don't remember.' He persisted with questions about whether she was frightened and about the reactions of the smaller children, to which she eventually replied, 'When the light went out and the children saw the blazes coming they all started crying.'

During the fire, many of the girls had shown remarkable courage. There was Una Smith, who went back up to the dormitory and thus saved Dolly Duffy's life; Dolly herself, whose shoes had been alight, picking up a badly injured child when the teacher, Miss Harrington, could not 'bring herself' to do so; Theresa Brady, who went 'back into the blazes' to drag out a younger child. There were those older girls, like Mary Lowry, who died trying to get the little ones out, and Mary

Caffrey, the sixteen-year-old 'non-pupil' who was given the key to the fire escape door by Sister Mary Clare, got up to the top storey through the terrible smoke and opened it. The only reaction to their bravery from the members of the tribunal was in a comment by the chairman to Mary Caffrey at the end of her evidence: 'You did your bit anyway, and you deserve praise for it.'

4

Report

The tribunal's report was published the following September. It was found that the fire was probably caused by a defective flue in the laundry and that the loss of life was caused by a combination of circumstances:

1. Fright or panic resulting in faulty directions being given.
2. Want of training in fire-fighting.
3. Lack of proper leadership and control of operations.
4. Lack of knowledge of the lay-out of the premises on the part of persons from outside.
5. Inadequate rescue and fire-fighting service and absence of light at a critical period.

A note was appended: 'While we are satisfied that more efficient and safer permanent means of escape could and should have been made available, we are not justified in finding that the absence of these contributed materially to the loss of life in the circumstances of this fire.'

Commenting on the role played by the fire brigade the report acknowledged that 'it is unfortunate that the members of the council and its advisers did not give fuller consideration to the rescue aspects. . . . We are satisfied that if they had done so it would have been possible to make a proper and timely effort to save the lives of the children.' Nonetheless, the tribunal added, 'we do not wish to suggest that the council was in any way avoiding its duty.'

In considering the evidence of the nuns the report stated: '. . . we feel bound to say that having heard the evidence of a number of the children trained and being trained in the institution, the relationship between them and the sisters seemed exceedingly happy, and that their demeanour and conduct. . . reflected credit on the Sisters in charge. . . . We are satisfied that. . . the Sisters did not consciously or willingly fail in any duty.'

The nearest the tribunal came in their report to laying blame for the disaster was in their comments on the behaviour of Miss O'Reilly.

Estimating the period of time during which the children could have been safely evacuated to be sixteen minutes from the discovery of the fire, they were 'satisfied' that, at the time when Miss O'Reilly returned to the upper two dormitories, it would have been possible for her and the adults in St Clare's to have brought the children in both dormitories to safety either down the wooden staircase or through the emergency door exit.

'Unfortunately, Miss O'Reilly in the excitement of the moment and in a state of fright, failed to do this. . . she committed a grave and critical error of judgement. . . . The circumstances were such as may have frightened a very timid person. She lost her head.' The report later recommended that the Department of Education should have a veto over the appointment of any teacher in an institution where 'such a person is proposed to be given charge of children at night.'

Finally, the report recommended that the rules for industrial schools and other government-regulated institutions should include provisions for proper fire escapes and more effective fire drill, and made proposals for covering the country with a modern fire-brigade network.

Forty years on, there are many people in Cavan and elsewhere who remember the fire. They wonder still why the simple, central issue was avoided by the members of the tribunal: what was the reason for the failure by the nuns either to get the children out of the dormitories themselves, or to give immediate orders to others to do so while there was still time? All the people to whom we spoke in the town, and all the girls we met who had spent their childhood in the orphanage, both before and after the fire, had always the same answer: that the first reaction of the Sisters, before they realised the seriousness of the situation, was to avoid themselves or the girls being seen in their nightclothes.

For this reason, it is believed, the girls were to be kept out of the way, and Miss O'Reilly was instructed to leave them in the dormitory. Ironically, it is quite possible that the children might have been taken out alive had the rescuers not appeared on the scene as early as they did.

Many local people believed that the dormitory doors were locked.[6] It would not have been considered unusual, at that time and in such a place. It was, after all, an industrial school, and an element of confinement was expected, particularly in a closed order. The report stated categorically that the dormitory doors were unlocked. It was apparent, however, from the evidence of the nuns, and from that of the girls and outside rescuers, that nearly every other door was locked and that the finding of keys and the unlocking of these doors consumed much valuable time.

The memory of Miss O'Reilly still arouses a hostile reaction. One of the rescuers who was present at the inquiry persists in his belief that she was 'covering up'. 'They kept asking her why, why did she put the children in the other dormitory, and she'd say, "I don't know". She must have been told to do it but wouldn't say so. Everyone thought that.' Miss O'Reilly was to remain in St Joseph's, sometimes in a supervisory capacity over the children when the Sisters went on retreats, for the rest of her life.

Two of the men who gave evidence at the inquiry recalled for us their memories of the girls. 'There was a big girl in the dock with the mentality of a child of five. She didn't know what to answer. She had to be taken away. All of them behaved younger than their years. Immature, that's what you'd call them; almost simple. There was one we knew because she used to run errands in the town. We congratulated her on the way she had given her evidence. "We were all rehearsed," she said.'

Louis Blessing is now portly and bald. He is considered to be 'a bit of a character' in the town. He owns a bar and shop in Pearse Street opposite the convent: he runs the bar, and there is a quiet woman in the shop, with its glass cases of Galtee processed cheese and iced cupcakes. He refused to talk about the fire. 'The place is all closed down now. What's the point?' When we asked what became of Cissie Reilly, he said nothing but gestured towards the shop, with a half-grin. The woman would say nothing either.

Later, we spoke to an old man who remembered industrial schools from the turn of the century and abhorred the system. 'It was fear,' he said, 'fear and too much discipline killed those children.'

Many of the men involved in the inquiry were later to reach prominent positions in public life. Mr John A. Costello, who appeared as Senior Counsel for the ESB, became leader of the first inter-party government in 1948 and was Ireland's Prime Minister from then until 1951 and from 1954-7. Mr T. F. O'Higgins, who appeared with him as Junior Counsel, twice ran as candidate for the presidency of Ireland,

and is now Judge of the European Court of Justice. Mr Tom Fitzpatrick, who appeared for two parents of children who had died, became a Minister in two Coalition governments and is Ceann Chomairle (Speaker) in Dáil Éireann. Mr P. J. Roe, who appeared for the Order, became a judge and his Junior Counsel, Mr Brian Walsh, became a Supreme Court Judge.

The secretary to the tribunal, Brian O Nualláin, was a man of many parts: as Myles na Gopaleen he was to become famous for his satirical column in the *Irish Times;* as Flann O'Brien, he was already, in 1943, the author of *At Swim Two Birds,* and as Brian O'Nolan he was known to innumerable Dubliners as wit and raconteur. Together with Mr T. F. O'Higgins, sitting in a bar in Cavan one evening during the inquiry, he composed the following limerick:

In Cavan there was a great fire;
Joe McCarthy came down to inquire
If the nuns were to blame
It would be a shame
So it had to be caused by a wire.

Neither the donations received by the Mother Abbess and the Bishop of Kilmore, nor the grief of the people of Cavan found expression in any memorial to the children. The grave in Cullies Cemetery where the thirty-five girls and the old woman lie is marked only by a granite coping and a small metal cross. On it is written 'In Memoriam to the Orphans who died in St Joseph's Industrial School, Cavan. May They Rest in Peace. Amen.' There are no names. There is no date.

Part Two

5

'One of the Good Schools'

These little children, who had not the care of their parents... had a beautiful substitute in the gentle protection of the sisters...

The Bishop of Kilmore, speaking at
the funeral service, February, 1943.

Ellen Neary today is a woman in her fifties with a sweet expression and a gentle manner. When she was three her mother died. A year later, in 1938, her father was found to have tuberculosis and he had to put Ellen and her two sisters into the orphanage. Sitting with us at the table in her spotless kitchen, exchanging polite formalities, suddenly she put down her sewing and covered her face with her hands.

'It was a hard place. It really was. I had a brother who died young, before my mother, and never went into an orphanage. I used often to think wasn't he the lucky one? I'd go into the chapel and pray to St Anthony to die. I had nothing to live for. The day my father left us, it was terrible. We cried our eyes out. So did he. I can still see us going through a door with glass in it. We were bathed and given our uniform – our prison clothes. When father was able, he'd come and bring us sweets. We used to show him the welts on our hands and tell him how we were treated. He'd cry and say "I know, I know". But sure what could he do?'

When they reached the age of twelve, the sisters were occasionally permitted to visit him in hospital. Then, one night, Ellen woke to hear the front-door bell ringing loudly through the orphanage. 'I knew then he was gone. They told me in the morning.' Her older sister – who was later to die in the fire – was allowed to go to the funeral, but Ellen was not. 'I got no comforting from any of the nuns. The only difference I knew was that Mother Carmel didn't beat me for a week.' (She was to discover later that her aunt in Scotland offered to take the three girls out of the school to live with her, but was refused. The reason given was that she was not a blood relation.)

Ellen and the two other women we met, Loretta MacMahon and Hannah Hughes, who had been in the orphanage at this time, have never forgotten Mother Carmel. She was a teaching nun but in the 1930s and early 1940s she had a supervisory role over the orphanage children – an era described by one as 'a reign of terror'. She was not the only one who beat them but there was an extra quality to her viciousness. As Ellen Neary put it, 'I sometimes think she must have been insane. She was a cruel, cruel woman. If the children didn't get up at 6.0 a.m., the minute she rang the bell in the dormitory, she'd pull back the bedclothes and flog them with a bamboo cane. Sometimes she'd hold back her sleeve and murder them on the bed, stripped, with the black strap. She was a devil.'

Loretta MacMahon recalled, 'I used to get up at five to escape her. That way I knew I'd be ready.' Hannah Hughes said, 'It was dangerous the way she'd hit you when you were still asleep. Poor Annie Hegney was beaten on the head with a bamboo cane and it got in her eye and it came up all swollen and sticking out.' Ellen Neary also remembered that 'Once when some of the children were linking arms in the playground, they crossed the line in the yard dividing the orphanage from the nuns' quarters. I pulled my sister back just in time. Mother Carmel called out all their numbers, took them upstairs, lined them up in a circle and went round and round beating their hands.'

Extract from Rules and Regulations for Industrial Schools, Punishment Section:

a) Forfeiture of rewards and privileges, or degradation from rank, previously attained by good conduct.
b) Moderate childish punishment with the hand.
c) Chastisement with the cane, strap or birch. This personal chastisement may be inflicted by the Manager or, in his presence, by an Officer specially authorised by him and in no case may be inflicted upon girls over 15 years of age. In the case of girls under 15, it shall not be inflicted except in cases of urgent necessity, each of which must be at once fully reported to the Inspector. Caning on the hand is forbidden. No punishment not mentioned above shall be inflicted.

But the girls had no knowledge of these rules designed to protect them, and Ellen used to hide her head under the bedclothes so as not to hear the screams of the smaller ones being beaten. 'It was hot one night and the little ones went to the bathroom for a drink. Mother Carmel found them out of bed and murdered them. I used to hate to see them being beaten. You'd hear them screaming and roaring.'

Many of the children wet their beds. It resulted in severe punishment. Ellen told us, 'There was a pot in one corner with screens round it, but some of the children would be too frightened to leave their beds in the dark. Sometimes they'd be put standing under cold showers and beaten but sure that only made it worse. If they wet the bed they got no food the next day, and if it happened again, no food for a second day.' Hannah said, 'I remember them watching us eating and we'd try to smuggle them a bit of bread even though we could hardly spare it.' One of her most vivid memories is of a child who was made to stand out in the yard in the cold for hours because she wet her bed. 'I can see her now, all huddled up, wearing a thin little dress and shivering. She died in the fire just before she was going off to become a nun. Mary Lowry was her name.'

> *Annual Report of the Department of Education, 1932: 'Only in its widest sense is the word discipline applicable. Methods adopted for character formation in Girls' Schools depend little on punishment and then of the slightest and briefest.'*

Hannah described the daily routine: 'We got up at 6.0 a.m., then a line of us would say our prayers, over to the washbasins, then the next line would come. Then over to the chapel – we had communion every day – and a lot of us used to fall asleep there. Then back to our duties, then breakfast which was shell cocoa made on water and a round of bread and margarine. There would be wriggling things on top of the cocoa but the boiling water would have killed them. 'We ate out of tin mugs and porringers. For dinner we had vegetables and potatoes, or a bowl of greasy soup with bits of bad potato. We had no meat except on Christmas Day or when the Inspector came. There were times when you'd see big rats running around the Refectory. We had lumpy stir-about made on oatmeal. We were always hungry. Sometimes we'd steal carrots and turnips and chew them raw in bed.' She said that at school the orphanage children used to go through the waste baskets to find lumps of bread left from the other children's sandwiches.' We were taught to make soda bread and we cooked meat, but we never got any of it.'

> *Rules for Industrial Schools: 'The children shall be supplied with plain wholesome food according to a Scale of Dietary to be drawn up by the Medical Officer of the School and approved by the Inspector. Such food shall he suitable in every respect for growing children actively employed and supplemented in the case of delicate and physically under-developed children with special foods as individual needs require.'*

The nuns, living in the convent, do not appear to have eaten the same food as the children. Ellen remembers getting the smell from their kitchen: 'It was so good it would make you feel faint. You'd go weak at the smell of eggs and bacon.' Hannah: 'We'd love working in the convent kitchen because we'd get their food.'

The son of the gardener employed by the community often helped his father in the vegetable garden. 'He grew asparagus, beetroots, peas, beans, tomatoes, cauliflower and early potatoes.' There was also a farm at the back, run by the steward. 'It produced milk and potatoes and he kept the hens. The eggs would have been for the convent, and the potatoes for the orphanage.' The nuns, he said with satisfaction, 'always had a very full table in the convent.'[1]

Each Friday night, the women said, the teaching nuns used to come over to the orphanage to bath the children, see that they changed their underwear and say prayers with them. Hannah remembers two or three children together in the bath. 'You'd be wearing a horrid wet shift that someone else had already used.'

The uniform of the 1930s, as remembered by Loretta, consisted of navy-blue rough serge dresses with pinafores and thick black stockings knitted in the orphanage, and hob-nailed boots. 'We had liberty bodices and our knickers were made out of flour bags. In summer we had a calico dress and sandals, but no ankle socks and never jumpers or cardigans.' Clothes were apportioned in a somewhat haphazard fashion. 'We'd put on whatever we could find and sometimes we'd end up with two left boots.'

A woman who attended the national school on the convent premises at this time remembered the orphanage children wearing unfashionably long dresses, never having jerseys, always looking frozen and having terrible chilblains. Ellen, Hannah and Loretta spoke constantly of the cold. 'We had no coats for years,' said Hannah and she recalled how they used to freeze in bed. 'There were great big windows and a cold wooden floor and five rows of beds. There was only one tiny fire in the place, and that was in the schoolroom.'

The women were conscious of how they must have looked. Hannah told us, 'If your hair got tangled they'd cut the bits out and never waited till you brushed it and it was always cut any old how . If a girl tried to put a little wave into her hair, they'd brush it back, as though there was something bad in you.'

Gifts of clothes and food were sometimes sent in for the children but they never – then or later – seem to have received them. Hannah said, 'I had an aunt in America who used to send us clothes, but we never got them. My mother used to come to see us once a month and bring us biscuits and sweets. We couldn't tell her how we were treated because the nuns would wait outside the door listening in case we'd tell her about the cruelty. She'd never have very long, they'd tell her she would have to go. Then they'd take the sweets and biscuits off us. I once got a little bag from Bishop Finnegan for being the best in class. It was satin and covered in beads. They took that off me as well and I never saw it again. We used to win medals for Irish dancing but they were used to make a crown for the Statue of Our Lady in the convent.'

Loretta had a similar memory. 'I won medals for singing and dancing in the Feis but I never got them. They went to make a halo for the Virgin Mary.' Entertainment of any kind was rare although Mother Carmel did occasionally put on a play. But, for the most part, the children were nearly as enclosed and cut off from the world as the nuns. The games they invented for themselves showed a remarkable similarity down through successive generations. Ellen remembers cutting dolls out of paper, dressing them with silver paper and putting them into matchboxes. By 1943 they must have had hoops to play with in the concrete school yard because their burned-out shapes were found after the fire.

In the summer they were allowed up the back into the convent fields. 'There were swings up there. We used to drink chestnut water made out of leaves, crushed up in water with a few grains of sugar.'

Under the 1908 Act children could be committed to industrial schools if they were orphaned, destitute, found begging or in need of care and protection. Their detention extended from the age of six to sixteen. After 1929 an amendment to the act permitted unmarried mothers to commit their children themselves, although it was not until 1939 that babies were admitted to St Joseph's. Before 1929, unmarried mothers and their babies would have gone to the County Homes, orphanages run by religious orders or to institutions catering specially for them, also run by religious orders. A notorious example of one of these was in Castlepollard, Co. Westmeath, where the young mothers were compelled to stay with their babies until they could be fostered out or sent to industrial schools.

Industrial School regulations permitted children to return home for a week's annual leave (extended to two in 1935), and the Department of Education's 1934 report noted that 'of an increasing number of pupils going home on a week's holiday, almost all return on the day fixed.' Hannah's widowed mother repeatedly asked if she could come out on holiday, but the request was always refused. No reasons were given.

Hannah was the youngest of a family of seven. Her father, who had a small-holding of a few acres in Cavan's rough, boggy hills, died when she was three. After a couple of years her mother could no longer support the family (this was before the advent of the widow's pension in Ireland), and she went to live with her father, taking the four older children with her. He could not take the three youngest girls and Hannah's mother had them committed to St Joseph's. The sisters rarely saw each other. They were kept apart in different groups, according to age.

Loretta MacMahon does not know who her parents were and has spent much of her life compulsively searching for her roots. She was told by a nun that she was about five years old when she came to St Joseph's, that she was illegitimate and was considered dull and backward. Like many who went through this and other institutions, she has no birth certificate. She has found this to be a constant obstacle and aggravation, whether for obtaining a passport, establishing pension rights or a claim to her home. Her attitude to her childhood is that however bad it was in the orphanage – 'like Charles Dickens' – life outside in those times was harsh too. 'But in there, it was life under duress.'

The picture of their childhood in the orphanage as told to us by the three women was almost unrelievedly harsh and bleak. Only Christmas seemed to bring a little colour into their lives. 'It was wonderful. People used to come in to serve us from the town. It was the only day we got enough to eat, it was the only day we enjoyed ourselves,' was how Hannah put it.

For Ellen it was more poignant. 'We used to look through the bars out into the street at the lights and the shop windows. We used to long for Father Christmas to come and leave something under our pillows. Once, my older sister got me a little sixpenny doll and wrapped it in a hanky. I was so thrilled.'

She said that some of the older children, accompanied by a lay teacher went out occasionally for a walk on Sunday, through the fields at the back, and sometimes to Lough Swellan. On Sundays and Holy Days they walked to mass in the cathedral. Some townspeople recollected their cleanliness and tidy appearance and told us that the children were looked after very well. Eugene Smith gave a more chilling description: 'They would huddle together; they didn't walk properly and held each others' hands as though for support. We never really thought about the orphans, though, they were just there, rather like the buildings. Those nuns should never have been put in charge of them. The children looked half-witted to me.'

A frequent comment we heard both in Cavan and elsewhere was: 'Sure the poor nuns were doing their best', or, 'If it wasn't for the nuns they'd have been out on the side of the street.' But John Kiely, one of Cavan's forty-one pub owners, felt differently: 'An enclosed order should never have been given the care of children.'

The girls did have contact with some of the town children who attended the national school. Some of them were from the 'Half Acre', a densely populated slum, and the fight against head lice was a continuous battle. Ellen: 'I couldn't work in the bathroom when they were doing the little ones' heads. I hadn't the stomach for it'. Older girls rigorously applied Jeyes Fluid, hot water and fine steel combs to little heads covered in scabs.

The town children were remembered as being very snobby. 'They looked down on us – we were just orphans.' But Hannah remembers one of the girls from Sullivan's bringing them in pieces of cut-up rhuharb and sugar: 'She knew we were starving.' One woman who had attended the national school said the town girls were not encouraged to associate with the orphanage children. 'They played separately, sat on different sides in class and we never knew their names. They really were pathetic but we envied them having hot cocoa at lunchtime, even though it was made with water.' She also remembered Miss Bridget O'Reilly as 'a thin woman with a hard, bony face and black hair in a roll.'

The orphanage children felt the lack of encouragement. 'The girls from the town were always being praised, but not us,' Loretta said. 'Everything I've learned, I learned by myself.' Ellen: 'How could you learn when you were afraid all the time? Mother Carmel used to say in class: "I'll get you afterwards!"'

The poor diet, poor hygiene and lack of care took their toll in health, and in life. Hannah remembers two of her friends dying from TB. 'I used to get boils on my head. My mother cried when she saw me. A nun burst one by hitting me on the head with a stick and the stuff ran down the side of my face. One morning Lizzie Brophy said she could not get up but Mother Carmel ordered her out although we kept saying she wasn't well. Lizzie kept crying that she had terrible pains, but Mother Carmel hit her with a black strap. When she did get up she fell on the floor and was taken to the Infirmary. They said she had rheumatic fever. The poor thing died a few weeks later. She was fourteen. God forgive me, but when I read about Belsen, I thought it was not much different.'

> *Annual Report of the Department of Education, 1928-9: 'Mortality rate 3.5 per thousand. This rate is somewhat higher than that for the country as a whole. Medical officers make quarterly inspections of all pupils and special attention is given to delicate pupils. Numbers under detention 6,515. Seven boys and sixteen girls died.'*

The regulations of industrial schools required that the children be 'respectful and obedient to all those entrusted with their management and training and to comply with the regulations of the schools.' A child over the age of twelve could, as a punishment, be sent to a certified reformatory school. Over the years, the threat of the laundry reformatories, run by orders of nuns who specialised in custodial care of 'wayward' girls and women, sometimes became a reality. There was Mary McHenry, for example. 'She used to comb her hair into a quiff.

The nuns would make her comb it straight again. One day she pulled off a nun's veil – I can't remember why – but we all thought it was good enough for her and we were delighted. But they sent Mary up to Dublin to a reformatory.' The same fate befell girls who tried to run away.

Hannah once successfully threatened a persecutor with higher authority. 'We were playing hide and seek, and one of the girls was under the bed when a nun came in and she heard her giggling. The nun told us to take off our clothes so that she could beat us and the other two did – though one of them was an adolescent and quite big – but I wouldn't. I said that my mother had told me to tell the Abbess if I was being ill-treated and she didn't touch me.'

Inspectors from the Department were required to make annual visits to each industrial school. It was their comments which were used in the compilation of the annual reports. At this time it was a Miss O'Neill who visited the girls' schools. Hannah recalled, 'They used to get a tip-off that the Inspector was coming. A lovely stew with meat would be put on to cook and we would be all cleaned up, and they would put counterpanes on the beds. The nuns used to load her down with chocolates and presents when she was going. Perhaps she got my bead bag! She hardly looked at the place.'

The nuns' lives then were very restricted and their regime severe. They would leave home as girls, expecting never to see their families again, not even to attend their parents' death-beds or their funerals. They were not permitted to leave their own convent until 1944 and then it was only to a sister house for many years. When they died they were buried in their own graveyard on the hill behind the convent. A local women told us how, if anyone rang the bell at the convent and a nun came to the door, she would have to talk standing sideways so that she could not see out into the street.

The names of the nuns whom the children loved for their kindness came up consistently. There was Mother Assumpta who spent years working alongside girls in the laundry, and Mother Scholastica and Mother Felix who, with older girls, took the babies from the Infirmary during the fire. Ellen can still hear Mother Assumpta saying that Mother Carmel would 'die three times for her cruelty'. It was always Mother Assumpta who used to smuggle extra food into the laundry. She would make an excuse to get a girl to come and help her and then give her a piece of bread and dripping. Mother Mary Clare also gave them food and sometimes even tea, a rare luxury. 'But even when you were little,' said Ellen, 'None of them would put their arms round you.'

The advent of a new nun affected dramatically the atmosphere of this small, closed-in world. 'When Mother Clare came we were dancing on air with freedom. When she gave us an orange we didn't know whether to eat the skin or the fruit. She gave us knives and forks, and we stopped lining up to get our food like Oliver Twist,' said Loretta.

In the opinion of the gardener's son the orphanage children were always well cared for. 'Sometimes my father would give them an apple or a tomato. I was once in Moate and saw an orphanage there run by the Sisters of Mercy. Sisters of No Mercy I called them! I saw a little girl of five or thereabouts in a thin dress put out in the frost and made to stand there on the concrete for a whole hour. The Poor Clares never did things like that.'

But the girls who had been to St Joseph's knew differently. Hannah: 'I've had nightmares about that place all my life.' Loretta: 'You've no idea what Christianity was like in those days. I've never been to church since.' And Ellen, a devout women who attends mass daily said, with tears in her eyes: 'I sometimes wonder how the nuns could have been so cruel to little children with no-one in the world to love them.'

6

'A Greater Affliction'

Under the terms of the Education Acts the girls at St Joseph's were supposed to stay at school until they were fourteen, but this was not always the case. Decisions seem to have been made about their future in a fairly arbitrary manner. Hannah, for example, thinks she was about thirteen when she was told one day that she was not going back to school. 'They put me to work in the laundry after that. We got up at 5.0 a.m. to wash the nuns' calico drawers and other things. One spot and they'd be thrown back at you and you'd get a clatter round the ear.' Each nun's washing would be in a separate bag and included soiled sanitary towels. 'We had to steep them first and then scrub them in cold water. It was terribly cold that water, your hands would always be red and raw. You'd boil them then, and, if they were badly stained, you'd have to put them on the bushes to bleach.' She also remembered having to tease out the nuns' hair mattresses and how all the hair would go into her mouth and nose.

Ellen said, 'The girls did all the cleaning, washing and cooking. I liked it at first, because it was something different to do, like helping to polish the brass in the chapel. Then we got tea and toast in the convent kitchen. It was lovely. Later on it all became just work. We'd be down on our knees, scrubbing and polishing, six in a line.'

After they reached the age of sixteen, even when their commital orders expired, some girls were kept on to sew or to work in the laundry. Mother Assumpta had eight girls of different ages working with her before the fire. Ellen was kept on until she was eighteen to do the extremely delicate and skilled embroidery and punch work – table mats, linen and underwear – which were sold by the Order. She said that she and the older girls who had been kept on to work sat at a separate table in the refectory and had tea for breakfast. 'They did not beat us when we were older. I suppose we were of more use to them then.'

Loretta, too, was clever with her hands. She said that from the age of about fourteen she worked in the sewing room, making the children's clothes, and she did a spell in the laundry too. The girls were thus receiving 'industrial' training as required in the rules, as they also were by scrubbing, cooking and polishing. 'There's one good thing you can say about all of us,' declared Hannah. 'We're all good housekeepers!'

When they finally left St Joseph's, most of the girls were sent out to work as domestics, either in hospitals or other institutions run by the many religious orders who provided much of the country's social and educational services. Too often they seem to have been badly exploited and were ignorant of their rights. Hannah remembers one girl who was sent to a farmer. 'She never got paid, and she had to do everything; milk cows, dig spuds, do housework. They worked her like a slave. She came back covered in abcesses. I'll never forget it. She went into hospital and died after a while. She was about twenty-two. It's terrible to think of it.' Hannah – a usually matter-of-fact woman – was visibly upset by the memory. She maintained that Mother de Salles told people not to pay the girls. 'Then Mother Mary Clare changed that. She wrote to people and made them pay.'

Ellen's elder sister was sent out on licence to an aunt who, like the rest of the family, had never come to visit her nieces.[3] 'She treated her like dirt and worked her like a slave. My sister asked me to see if I could get the nuns to take her back in again.' Ellen said that the two Galligan sisters who died in the fire had gone out to work but had also asked to come back because they were so harshly treated.

Department of Education Annual Report, 1936: 'All the schools have more applications for employment than girls to place. Reports of the capability and conduct of the girls in employment testify to the value of training and the care given in school and afterwards.'

Department of Education Annual Report, 1933: 'Careful investigation has shown that the rate of wages paid to girls who left the schools and trustworthy reports of their industry and character testify to the maintenance of the good records of the preceding years.'

A very different version of life in the orphanage came to us from Constance Henry, one of the girls who survived the fire and who later became a nun. She wrote us a letter in which she said that she was put into St Joseph's as a dying wish of her mother. She was four when this happened, and her mother was frightened that her only daughter would be taken by relatives who would work her too hard. 'My earliest recollections of the place are of a Caring and Loving group of Nuns. . . I was fortunate in being placed under a Sister Mary Byrne who knew my family well. . . she told me I used to kick and scream if I could not have a pretty dress, very short and often sleeveless. . . I have no recollections of ever being dressed in "drab" uniform. I dare say my temper would have exploded if I had. . . A Mother de Salles was in charge of all the girls and was a kindly, very concerned person. She had a close liaison with our family as I learned later from my Father. . . Then there was Sister Mary Clare from around 1936.

'Looking back on her reign I feel her main emphasis was "Further Education" once we completed the National School. . . With the assistance of two lay teachers she organised domestic science classes, dressmaking, knitting, needlework, embroidery, cookery classes and laundry work. . . We competed for the annual Cavan show when I was fifteen, and I landed a first, second and third prize for various knitted garments and the teachers were just as excited as I was. She inspired us with a desire and love of reading and in the long winter Sunday evenings, she had a store of books to choose from – novels, short stories, magazines, religious books and lives of the Saints. . . We learned singing – Irish, English and Plain Chant. . . Each year and on a special occasions we had a Concert for the nuns and relations consisting of drama, opera, dancing and singing and all enjoyed these. . . In summer we had P.E., netball, egg and spoon race, sack race and ball games and annually had a Games Day. . . Up the hill we had swings and other amusements and a large shed to store hoops, skipping ropes, balls, chairs and this sheltered us when the rain fell.

'The day commenced with a call at 7.30 by one of the nuns. Wash – morning prayers and then breakfast at 8.0 to 8.30. We each had a little chore to do after breakfast until 9.0 a.m. in which Sister supervised. Assembled at 9.0 a.m. to wash and dress for school. . . We had frequent Fire Drill Lectures at, I believe, three monthly intervals and we were well acquainted with the routes to take if fire occurred. . . Under-eights and those who suffered nocturnal eneuresis in St Clare's dormitory with a senior girl in charge and some fifteen and sixteen-year-olds to help her get the little ones to the toilet at night. . . I have no recollections of ever going hungry. . . the food was plain but it must have been sufficient to sustain us. Those of us who had relatives and parents did go on holidays annually and our parents and relations visited us. . . The Poor Clare Nuns, whom I was privileged to know were great, noble, saintly women, who inspired us towards good and beautiful ideals.'

We know little of what became of most of the girls who passed through the orphanage during that era before the fire. Certainly Ellen, Hannah and Loretta all married and made something of their lives in time. Even so, Hannah was tense with worry until all her children were grown and independent. 'I was so frightened for them – frightened that anything would happen to me or my husband and they would go through what I did. I scrimped and saved and knitted and sewed and I made them do their homework and, thank God, they've all done well.'

Ellen, too, was constantly fearful that she or her husband would die before their children were settled. 'I used to be ashamed to say I was from the orphanage, and I burnt all the cuttings about the fire and the photo of me standing by the grave, but I'm sorry I did now.' To Loretta, now living in England, 'the shame of that place' was something from which her husband had helped her to hide. 'I've spent all my life escaping from the orphanage, and I've succeeded too!'

Apart from their 'industrial training', the girls appear to have received no preparation for the world outside the convent walls. The usually complacent Department of Education reports had noted this, and observed in 1925 that 'The standard of training and the preparation of pupils to be self-reliant in after life is much in need of improvement.' Despite this, the three women said they received no information on 'the facts of life'. They were not prepared for menstruation, for which they were given a piece of lint-like cloth that had to be washed. As Ellen put it, 'You could almost say we were a bit simple – why, we never even knew what age we were!' Hannah said, 'We didn't know the difference between right and wrong. A lot of the girls went astray when they left. I don't know how many fell. Something stopped me. I had a fear of getting into trouble myself, though I didn't even know the facts of life until I was twenty-one. Just imagine that! I was working as a domestic and I came down the stairs in the dark and there was this man who used to deliver things to the house – the dirty thing! That was the first time I'd seen a man's body. There was a nice, odd-job man, an old bachelor, who worked round the house who was very kind to me, and when I told him what happened he explained things to me.'

'They were half simple. A lot of the girls went wrong afterwards,' said John Kiely, the pub-owner. Eugene Smith thought that a lot of them 'fell' when they left and, according to Hannah, two of the girls 'fell' before they left the convent walls. One girl, she said, had a baby by a man working there, another was assaulted 'up in the garden' and 'there was a girl had a baby by a soldier soon after she left'. We heard of another who had a baby within a year of leaving the orphanage, and had spent the rest of her life as a priest's housekeeper, and of 'poor Annie Hegney' whose eye was injured by Mother Carmel, and who later married a local man who drank, beat her and gave her no money for her children's food.

We tried to find 'poor Katy O'Toole'. We had heard about her from several of the girls of later years. They said she was sent straight from St Joseph's to the Magdalen Home in Galway. There, apparently, she was 'detained' for twenty-one years until, during the 1950s, her sister happened to tell a Dublin doctor, for whom she was working, about her. He went to Galway and got Katy out. The girls said that when they knew her – she used to visit the orphanage – she was 'a bit simple'. It was at this Magdalen Home that unmarried mothers and mothers-to-be had their heads shaved to ensure that they would not leave. Katy is thought to be working in the kitchens of another clerical institution somewhere.

Sister Constance, in her letter, said that four years after the fire 'I fulfilled my childhood ambition and entered a Convent in England.' She said she was 'well, happy and able to do a good day's work. . . The great spirituality implanted in me by my parents and sustained and nurtured by these great nuns in Cavan is my best asset in my work with the sick. . . When reading, studying or listening to lectures on psychology and the detriment to people's characters caused by "institutional upbringing", I really have a good laugh, because Thank God I seem to have escaped all these effects and I feel, and have felt, a contented, happy person.'

When Hannah left the orphanage, all she had were the clothes she stood up in and a packet of sanitary towels. 'I left on my sixteenth birthday. My mother came to collect me and we went and had tea in the town and then went home. I'll never forget going out of that door.' She spent two weeks with her mother and then went off to a job as housemaid in Dublin. She married at twenty-five a man who, she says, has always been good to her. They live in a scrubbed-clean little house in Co. Galway. She has lost her religion.

Ellen left the orphanage in 1942. She was given a winter coat, a beret, two interlock vests and two pairs of knickers. She went to work as a live-in alteration hand for six shillings a week and soon met her husband. 'I have told him and my children all about my childhood. I think that's why they are so good to me, because it was so sad. I suppose the worst thing was looking through the bars of the windows to the street and feeling so lonely, knowing there was nobody to come for you.'

For nine days during the year, they told us, and for three days before Christmas there had to be total silence in the orphanage when the nuns went on retreat. We wondered how small children could be kept quiet for so long. Ellen considered the question for a moment. 'Fear,' she said, 'Fear will make you do anything.'

> *Department of Education Annual Report, 1943: 'A serious outbreak of fire which unfortunately resulted in the death of 36 persons. . . took place at St Joseph's Industrial School, Cavan, in the early morning of 24 February, 1943.'*

7

'A Substitute For The Family Life'

Annual Report of the Department of Education, 1946: 'A new building at Cavan of modern design and with up-to-date equipment to replace the Industrial School building destroyed by the fire in February 1943 has been completed and will provide accommodation for 100 children.'

Eugene O'Brien told us, 'There was a fine building put up after the fire. I saw around it myself – a grand place, I remember looking at all the toilets and there were small ones for the babies going up to big ones for the older children. Everything was better after the fire. It cleared up a lot of things. The girls had a better time – they were around the town quite a lot, but you'd have to work at it to get them to talk to you.'

Two elderly nuns whom we talked to referred to everything as 'before' or 'after' the fire. 'Everything changed after. . . children were allowed out without escort. They were allowed to visit, allowed to go and help at the Bishop's house. After 1943 we were amalgamated with Newry – before that we were never allowed out of the convent. Things got so much better after the fire that it was almost a blessing in disguise.'

Rosemary Tracey was sent to the orphanage a few months before the fire. She was twelve years old at the time and grieving for her mother who had just died, 'Mother had been ill in hospital for ten months and I'd always said that if she died, I'd die too. I felt I wanted to go and drown myself. I suppose they did not know what to do with me, the way I was, and my older sister would have been busy looking after the younger ones. They must have thought the nuns could do something for me. Anyway, they put me in the orphanage.'

She found it difficult at first, she said, but she made friends. Then, almost immediately, she lost them in the fire. 'Nothing seemed the same after. It was so strange without them. Remembering them every time you went into the yard. I was unhappy in the new building and I felt closed-in in the new playground. It was so lonely without the other girls.'

Sally Johnson was put into the orphanage as a baby in 1940 and left in 1955 at the age of sixteen. Her memories were often, word for word, the same as those of the previous generation in the 1920s and 1930s.

'We lived off porridge, bread and potatoes. We ate off metal dishes and drank out of enamel mugs. We had two slices of bread and cocoa made on water for breakfast. In the autumn a farmer brought in apples – that was marvellous. The favourite job was to take up the gardener's tea. He'd give you a tomato or something if you put in extra sugar. The best dinner was on Sunday: we got a nice pudding with jam and rhubarb and custard and tea. We all loved tea. After a while we got sausages every Saturday. I still remember the first time it happened. The butcher came up to kill a pig now and again and we had pig stew for ages. Everyone loathed it. They killed it right there in the yard – we didn't mind that – it was the stew we hated, all greasy. They'd only give us the fatty bits anyway. We'd eat the vegetable peelings – turnips and such – out of the pits in the garden. The chickens got better food than us – we used to take their food.'

Department of Education Annual Report 1949: 'Dietary scale subject to careful scrutiny. . . minimum of one pint of milk per day.'

'In the summer we wore gingham dresses and jumpers and skirts in the winter. Miss O'Reilly – Fag O'Reilly we called her – made the clothes. Under the dresses we wore chemises and a bodice and a grey flannel petticoat and thick black stockings. A pile of shoes was taken out in a heap, and you got what you could and hoped it fitted. I once had a pair two sizes too small for months. I can remember that a girl from the town had different socks and dresses every day for school and we were so envious. But there were great facilities: it wasn't until I came to live in England that I saw an outside toilet.'

Sally reckons there to have been around ninety girls in the orphanage at that time.[4] Each girl had a number: hers was no. 13. When she was six she started to help to clean out the convent chapel. 'I thought it was exciting at first. Not later on. We cleaned out the rooms, corridors, classrooms. We swept, dusted and scrubbed. Paying for our mothers' sins I suppose. As we got older the nuns didn't treat us so roughly because they relied on us more for work. But there is one thing I'll never forget because it was so upsetting: Mother Bernadette got Lal Smith sent to the reformatory in Limerick. Lal – why, she was only twelve at the most – and she was always good for a giggle, kept us in fits. She never did wrong, nothing wrong at all. Poor Mother Assumpta, how she cried about it. Fag O'Reilly used to threaten to send us to Limerick too. But Mother Carmel was worst of all. She was a wicked, wicked woman. I was petrified of her. She used to beat me so much and for the three years I was in her class I wet the floor – Mother Assumpta would always dry my drawers. I hate to say it but I think Carmel must have been a sexual deviant.'

Bridget Rooney was born in the same year as Sally Johnson but she did not go into the orphanage until she was twelve, in 1953. Her mother had died and her father committed his two daughters to St Joseph's and his two sons to Artane. They never saw him again. 'I remember Inspector O'Connor bringing us to Cavan on a train. "It's going to be a nice place," he said. A couple of months later he came to see if we were all right. I was dressed up in my best clothes, but two nuns sat with me while he was talking to me. I wanted to tell him about the place but I was too frightened.'

'We were treated like a herd of cattle, brought up like animals. We always sat in the back seats at school and we were called "orphans". We knew the other children at school were better than us, but I came from a nice home. In that way it was worse for me than for my younger sister, because I could remember. Anyone that wasn't good at school was taken out to work in the orphanage. They did that to me when I was thirteen. We got up at 5.0 a.m. and every day we had to go to mass at 6.0 a.m. I had to wash and starch all the nuns' clothes and habits. My fingers used to be bleeding. And we had to scrub miles of corridors. We went to bed at 7.30, even the big girls. Children were locked up as a punishment, sometimes for two days with nothing to eat. Mother Andrew did that. She was the most vicious woman I ever met in my life. She would break up orange boxes and beat us across the back. I know some girls were scarred for life by what happened to them in Cavan. Fear was inside of you all the time.'

Jane and Eilis grew up in Cavan town and went to St Joseph's national school. Jane, who came from a professional family, was there from 1947-51. 'The orphans were sad and miserable-looking. They had a smell as though they had wet themselves, mixed up with disinfectant and an aura of fear. They always looked cold as though they didn't have enough underneath their calico dresses. You were always aware that they were different. The nuns created this by segregating them and by beating them more than the rest of us. You were never supposed to get friendly with them, and they weren't allowed even to play with us at break – they had to go back to the orphanage. You'd never hear them laughing or larking around. We all knew something was wrong about the way they were treated and we felt sorry for them.'

Eilis's background was also middle-class. She attended the national school from 1950-3, between the ages of eight and eleven. 'Some of the children in my class were still scared from the fire. We used to see the older ones looking after the smaller children: they were like mothers to them. I went to that school from a small Protestant country school and I was shocked by the corporal punishment. Mother Carmel was the most incredibly cruel woman I have ever met. She always carried a cane strapped on to her waist beside her crucifix. Once she took a girl away into a room to beat her – she was a simple girl with a big vacant face – and I said, "You can't beat her," and ran after them. She turned to me and said, "You'd get it too if it wasn't for who you are."'

Eilis said that many people from the town had taken their children away from the school after the fire but they began to drift back gradually because of the nuns' more enlightened approach. 'The orphans were well-dressed then, better almost than we were. I remember going over to the orphanage and noticing their toys. I rather envied them really. My strongest memory is of being sent to the orphanage to fetch something and seeing a family coming in. There were about four children with their father. He looked completely dazed and the children had looks of absolute horror on their faces. I shall always remember it. I said to the nun, "Who are they? Where do they come from?" and she replied, "We never know the backgrounds of the children who come in here." There was a big poster in the orphanage with the caption "The Family Who Prays Together Stays Together". Even at the time I thought it was an odd place to have it.'

Department of Education Annual Report 1953: 'During the School year, on the advice and with the approval of Dr McQuaid (Archbishop of Dublin) arrangements were made by members of the

Religious Orders conducting Industrial Schools for the establishment of a short course in child care for Managers and Sisters in charge of Children's Homes. . . . There is every reason to believe that among the benefits of this course will be further improvement in school standards, the increased welfare and happiness of the children in the schools and a better preparation of them for life.[5]

Most of our information on life in St Joseph's came from thirteen girls born between 1946 and 1954. Some were put in as babies, none after the age of four. Many of them think they were illegitimate. Some we met several times, others only once. From another, now living in Australia, we received a letter. Several whom we tried to contact refused to talk to us. In all essentials the memories of the girls we met corroborated each other. Only details differed. Inevitably the dominant impressions were created by the surrogate mother-figures who supervised them.

Mothers Bernadette and Andrew appear to have been in charge until the mid-50s. Unpleasant incidents involving Mother Andrew were often mentioned, but Mother Bernadette was remembered with affection by this age group, who were very young during her tenure, if not by those who were older.

Tina Martin, born in 1951, told us, 'Mother Bernadette was nice, I'm sure. I remember going hand-in-hand up the yard with her, and her giving us a smartie each and telling us to look at the stars.' Maureen Harty said, 'Mother Bernadette was marvellous. We were all individuals to her.' Ann-Marie Hanley, born in 1947, remembered, 'You could go to Mother Bernadette with your arms out if you were crying.' Perhaps her kindness – even love – towards them was due to the fact that she had looked after them when they were small. Even from Sally, whom she persecuted, we got this picture of her, 'The babies had their food made up by Mother Bernadette. She would mash in a soft boiled egg into potatoes, all on one platter, and then go with one spoon round the circle of them, their mouths opening like little birds.'

Elizabeth Bright told us, 'You felt free with Mother Bernadette. You could run round in your bare feet. You could go to her if you hurt yourself. When she left there were about sixty of us holding on to the railings, crying at the gate. And then *they* came. Mother Anne and Mother Catherine. With them it was a reign of terror.'

These two nuns appear to have been in charge from the mid-50s to the mid-60s and Mother Anne, according to several of the girls, immediately set about improving their living conditions. Ann-Marie recalled, 'When she first came we had terrible old rags of clothes and she made everyone of us – there were about fifty of us then, though my number was still no. 70 because you held on to your number regardless – blouses and maroon-coloured pinafore dresses, all pleated. She got a nun in Gormanstown to make us all jumpers with lovely warm collars. They were really very smart. Each of us had different colours so that we wouldn't look the same. We were never allowed to have long hair before she came but she let all the children's hair grow and she got us lovely ribbons. It was a complete new way of life for us. She got swings put up and gave us balls to play with. Before that you'd be told to go out and play and you'd have nothing to do.'

Frances Devaney, born in 1950, told how Mother Anne would stay up all night sewing: 'One Christmas I got a navy dress with green socks. I was so thrilled.' A social worker who had worked in Co. Cavan at about this time also remembered how she had divided up the dormitories into cubicles for the girls.

But even though, materially, the girls' lives had improved, their punishments remained severe and out of all proportion to their wrongdoing. Many of them had particular incidents – sometimes when another child was the victim – which stood out in their mind, never to be forgotten. Nora said, 'The worst time was when I was sent to fetch the strap after breakfast for Deirdre Ryan. I was shaking all over and I wondered what the girls would think of me for getting it, but what could I do? I remember Deirdre saying, "No matter what she does I'm not going to cry." "Oh," says Mother Anne, "so you're not going to cry are you?" She walloped her and walloped her and we were all bursting out crying and saying, "Deirdre, please cry! Oh, please cry!" But she wouldn't and in the end she was let go.'

Several of the girls remembered that occasion, as they did another involving Mother Catherine. They would mention it again and again, almost incredulously. Nora said, 'Mother Catherine came in one day with a big box of sweets. She called us all together and told us to take a big handful each. Just one sweet was a treat to us and we just couldn't believe it. The little ones were staring at her. When we'd all taken them, Mother Catherine said, "Now you can put them all back again. I've made right fools of ye." How could anyone have been so cruel to children? I've never forgotten it. None of the girls have.'

Elizabeth told us, 'Catherine, she had a horrible mind. God forgive me, but she shouldn't have been a nun. Ann-Marie and I had to look after little twin babies when we were about eleven, I suppose, and feed them at night. "Who fed the babies?" she asked the next day. I stood up and she said, "And I suppose you fed the boy?" She sent someone for the wooden spoon. I know I got sixty slaps because I counted. It was so unjust that I decided to run away. I got as far as the courtyard door when Catherine came running after me, begging me to come back. I said I would go to the police if they hit me again, and she said they wouldn't. After that they only hit me when I wet my bed. But when I was thirteen or fourteen Mother Anne called me up because I had put a pair of stockings belonging to an older girl to dry on a radiator and we weren't supposed to do that. She slapped me with the cane again and again. My wrist turned a horrible colour, yellow but no blood. It hurt dreadfully. I went up to bed where she'd sent me and lay there with my wrist out so that everyone could see how awful it looked. Mother Anne came in and thought I was asleep and I heard her gasp out, "Good God, what have I done here? God, I couldn't have done it." She sent up a girl to get me down to dinner and I got a second helping for the first time in my life. Otherwise the only time we got enough was at Christmas.'

Connie Fitzpatrick, born in 1947, went to the orphanage when she was almost three: 'I wish I could know who I was or if I was illegitimate. It would put my mind at rest.'[6] Other girls spoke of Connie as being popular with the nuns and well treated by them. She told us she had loved the orphanage. 'Mother Anne was fond of me. She always called me by my Christian name. They were good to me but I've seen what I've seen – girls getting lashed on their bare bottoms. Once a crowd of us were hanging out of the central heating pipes pretending to be monkeys and Mother Anne came down and caught us. She was carrying a pile of wood like as if she had broken up a box for firewood. She hit me with a piece of it and when she tried to pull it away she couldn't because there was a nail stuck right into my hand. She pulled and pulled, and there was blood everywhere. Then she threw all the sticks down and brought me upstairs and bandaged me up and she was. . . kind of crying.'

Connie used to help to look after the younger children when she was ten or eleven. 'Sometimes there'd be around twenty of them, five- or six-years-olds. I felt sorry for the nuns a lot of the time. They had an awful lot to do looking after us.'[7]

Maureen Harty was born in 1940. She was greatly admired by the other girls because she was so pretty. She had, at first, refused to talk to us – 'I would go out of my mind if I had to think about that place' – but later she changed her mind. Mother Catherine dominated her memories which were mainly of constant, pointless beatings. She suspected that this nun was jealous of her long golden hair: 'Once when it was all tied up in a pony tail, she cut it off by the elastic.' Maureen said she was constantly nervous: 'I hated to hear my name called for fear I'd done something wrong and would be beaten.[8] Once we had this white stuff to eat – I suppose it was macaroni or tapioca – and it made me sick. I was made to eat the vomit and was sick again.' She said that in school all thefts were blamed on the orphanage children: '"Come up to the front, you orphans, and turn out your pockets!" I knew all the time that we looked awful. We wore boys' boots with a tag at the back.'

Although many of the older girls behaved like mothers to the younger children, sometimes forming a particular attachment to them, a few of the girls contributed in their own way to the 'reign of terror', repeating what they had seen done to others. Maureen remembered, 'Some of them were very cruel. If you wet your bed they'd put you under a cold shower and beat you.' Tina said, 'The stronger ones beat us and bullied us. I was terrified of Sheila Delaney. She would suddenly hit at you really violently.' Tina was fond of Deirdre Ryan, several years younger than herself. 'I told her to call me in the night and I'd carry her to the toilet.'

The two youngest girls we met were the Ryan sisters, Margaret, born in 1953 and Deirdre a year later. Because they were only ten months apart they were not, as usual, separated in the orphanage. Deirdre thinks that they were born in England and that their mother, who was unmarried, went to work in a factory leaving them with a baby-sitter. She imagines they were neglected because the RSPCC took them away and sent them first to the Poor Clares' home for babies in Stamullen, and then to St Joseph's when they were three. Two years later, said Deirdre, their mother came to see them. 'It's as clear as yesterday. She gave us sweets and biscuits and I was so excited I wet my pants. The nuns were mad and they took away the things and made me stand in a corner. We saw her again for the last time when I was seven. She was wearing a brown hat and coat.'

'Margo and me were always being beaten but we stood up for each other. I was real wild and I used to jump out of windows and climb trees. I was sent to a psychiatrist because I wasn't learning at school – I can write a little but I wouldn't be able to read out loud. They used to clatter me for this the whole time, even when the doctor told them I shouldn't be hit. But I was sick a lot of the time and when you were ill I must say they'd look after you well.'

Margaret is quieter and more thoughtful than Deirdre. 'I think our mother used to send us sweets and things. Once she came to see us. I think I was seven or eight but the nuns never said she was our mother. I've always held that against them. The posh people would be shown into the parlour when they came, but our mother was kept standing out in the yard. I remember how cold it was. I think she may have wanted to take us away because the nuns said, "Do you want to go?" and we said, "No!" Nothing was ever explained to us. I'd love to find my mother. I used to think about her a lot, especially at Christmas, but I wouldn't interfere with her. After all, she might be married and her husband not know about us.

'Deirdre was terribly delicate: she used to get Ribena to drink. I'd have to get her dressed in case the nuns would murder us for being late. Her fingers used to be hanging down with broken chilblains and yellow stuff coming out. I remember her once screaming out my name and when I rushed up into the dormitory two of them had her on the bed and they were beating her. They had Mother Benedict with them. She was a teaching nun – maybe they brought her over for a kick, excuse my saying it.

'Nora O'Hanlon was very good to us. She'd hide us behind her so that the nuns would hit her instead of us. If Mother Anne or Mother Catherine called us into the workroom I would be holding on to the wall with fear. Deirdre and I were sent to a psychiatrist once. He watched us playing for a while and then he asked us if we wet our beds. We were mad and said we didn't. He said Deirdre was a bit wild, but that we were both quite normal.'

Nora has vivid memories of the orphanage: of picking gooseberries and strawberries in the nuns' garden – 'We didn't get given any, only what we stole' – of standing outside the nuns' kitchen savouring the smell. 'Their dog Wopsey did too. He never bothered with our kitchen.' Like Ellen Neary, thirty years earlier, she described getting chestnut leaves, putting them into bottles with water and a few grains of sugar, then shaking it and drinking it. 'We'd collect buckets of leaves out of the hedges and eat them like mad. I've often wondered since if that was why we were so healthy. Sometimes one of the girls would get sent in oranges and we'd fight over the skins. We'd put our hands down the drains in case maybe the national school kids would have dropped pennies by mistake, and if ever we found one we'd go to Sullivan's or Hickey's and buy sweets.[9] We didn't like the holidays much because we had nothing to do. On Saturday mornings we used to sit in the yard taking the white part off silver paper or shredding material – teasing, we used to call it. I suppose it was for pillows and things.'

'The girls from Cavan were always very clean. We had a bath once a week. We'd stand in a line in our knickers, giggling at the girls who had big chests. We wore big drawers that came down to our knees. Each week they had to be inspected before we got clean ones. We used to stand at the end of our beds holding out the knickers and shaking with fright, and then the nuns would call you a dirty thing in front of everybody. It was cruel, it really was.'

Hunger and cold were repeated themes, even from this generation of girls. In the 1960s they were still rooting for food in the hen buckets and fighting over scraps of burnt porridge. Mary said, 'We were always cold. We weren't allowed cardigans until it got really cold and I used to be shivering in my summer frock. When you wet the bed, you'd be made to sit on the toilet for ages in the dark.' Ann-Marie agreed, 'It was cold, always cold. We used to get dreadful chilblains. There was a pipe in the yard where the hot air used to come out from the laundry. We used to huddle in by the pipes and one girl would be warming her hands while another sat on the pipes to dry her knickers.'

A local woman recalled, 'I used to go to early mass, quarter to seven in the mornings. Prayer has always been a great comfort to me. The orphans used to be there in the freezing cold without any socks on, just sandals and short-sleeved frocks, shivering and yawning with being tired. Sometimes they'd be kept waiting for half an hour if the priest was late.

Sometimes you'd see them faint. The parish has bought the chapel now from the nuns and it's always centrally heated. It breaks my heart seeing all the heat going to waste when you think how cold the little children were for so long and how they were never there to enjoy it.'

There were always good, kind nuns. A figure who glows through their stories from the 1930s until the orphanage closed was Mother Assumpta, working uncomplainingly down in her laundry. Frances told us, 'Sometimes you'd see her staggering up the steps with two big pails of water and we'd all run to help her. She had to work so hard and we all loved her.' Elizabeth said, 'Mother Assumpta was marvellous. If I could get my sheets to her in the laundry in time, she'd have them washed and dried so that I wouldn't get the strap for wetting my bed. She used to cry when she heard the children screaming.'

Other nuns, too, were remembered with affection, particularly one who came as a substitute when Mother Anne and Mother Catherine went away for a few weeks. 'You could not believe there was such a friendly nun,' said Mary. 'She bought us new dresses and underwear and we had a fry in the evening and were allowed to stay up late. She must have had them in debt by the time she left.' Tina told us, 'Mother Paschal was hard and cross, but at the same time she would give you sixpence and say, "Get yourself some sweets." Once she organised a concert for us and the Mother Abbess gave us a big feed afterwards.'

This Mother Abbess, Mary Joseph, unlike her predecessors, was often mentioned by this group of girls. They would run to her, carry things for her and talk to her whenever they could. According to Tina she loved music and arranged for a few of the girls to have free violin lessons.

Connie thinks it was this Abbess who introduced the 'godparent' system. She was given a woman she calls Auntie Dot, who used to visit her sometimes on Sundays: 'I used to think perhaps she was my mother.' Margaret Ryan was given a godmother who wrote to her every week and sent her sweets and comics. Gradually the children were coming into contact with the outside world. Many of them went on holiday to relatives and they were allowed to visit the homes of the girls who went to the national school.

In 1961 the Poor Clares had their Centenary Jubilee which was attended by the prime minister, Mr de Valera. The celebrations included an entertainment provided by the children, and a dinner.

But Christmas and the annual outing remained the highspots of each year. Nora recalled, 'Christmas was really great. We sang at midnight mass and we had rashers and eggs for breakfast. They were cooked the night before but we didn't mind. Then we had a big dinner served by the nuns who waited on us and the priests came in too. They really gave us the best: we had turkey, ham, plum pudding, biscuits and sweets. At three o'clock we got our parcels. Santa Claus called out our names. He really looked the thing up on the stage and we all got presents and tiny things out of a huge cracker. There were plenty of children in the town who didn't have half what we did at Christmas. At Easter Mrs Hickey who had the sweet shop across the road made a huge big egg out of plaster of paris and it would be full of little eggs.'

'The outing was always in the summer. We might go to Virginia or Gormanstown, and we'd be given a classroom in some school to eat our sandwiches in. Once or twice a year the boy scouts would come in from the town and do a play for us. We loved that.

Mother Anne and Mother Catherine were replaced, in the mid-60s, by Mother Theresa and Mother Cecilia and happier times followed. As Margaret said, 'They made things better for us. But they always separated the ones with parents from the ones without in the way they treated us. If your father was someone, you'd get more. Theresa used to hit us but she was good all the same. We were allowed to watch the telly and Mother Cecilia would buy us ice pops on Sundays and we'd get marmalade with our bread and margarine for breakfast. On our birthdays she would make us a cake with candles on it and give us a holy picture and two sweets in an envelope. I suppose there were too many of us to give us love. I think the nuns honestly believed that they were doing good and would make us better by beating us. "If it wasn't for us, you'd all be on the side of the road," they'd often say.'

In 1957 the Poor Clare nuns opened a free secondary school,[10] built on their premises. It would, therefore, have been possible for the orphanage children to have continued their education until their committal orders expired and to have improved their chances of getting jobs, other than as domestic servants, which the majority of them became. But many of this generation of girls were actually kept out of school to work in the convent or to look after the babies during the day and feed them at night. Of the thirteen girls born after 1945 whom we interviewed, four were illiterate when they left St Joseph's and three other girls told us that they were the only orphanage girls ever to be sent to the secondary school.

Annual Report of the Department of Education, 1959: 'The great majority of the children under detention are committed to the schools on the grounds of lack of proper guardianship, and the efforts of the school authorities are directed towards providing, as far as possible, a substitute for the family life. . . .'

'Lack of proper guardianship' is a legal term. There were conflicting opinions over the years as to whether it was the industrial school manager or the Department of Education who was *in loco parentis* for committed children. It seems to have been in the mid-50s that not only the industrial school regulations but also the law of the land began to be broken and broken in a manner injurious to the children by those into whose care they had been given for this proper guardianship. Firstly, they were taken out of school before the minimum leaving age. Secondly, they were sent away to work – both below the school leaving age and before their committal term was up. Thirdly, several of the girls were sent to a non-certified, extra-legal reformatory.

Cissie Meehan entered the orphanage aged four. 'I was delicate so I didn't get much schooling. I had an awful cough and was in bed a lot. I don't think I went to school much after I was nine. They probably thought I had missed too much so they put me in the nuns' kitchen.' Ann-Marie remembered Cissie as someone who had no-one and who was given a harder time than most, both in the way she was beaten, sometimes just for looking grubby, and in the way she was worked. 'We used to feel sorry for her when we'd see her all greasy-looking, carrying two big slop buckets for the pigs up the iron stairs from the nuns' kitchen and then up more steps to the farm. It can't have done her much good if she was delicate.' When she was thirteen, Cissie was sent away to work as a domestic in Dublin.

Joan was sent out to work at the age of twelve. She maintains she was always brought back to the orphanage when the medical inspector's visit was imminent in case her absence would be noted.[11] This visit took place once a year. Ann-Marie had reason to remember it. 'I was about ten and I was after getting a hiding and I was covered in marks. The doctor came unexpectedly and we all had to take off our clothes to be examined. Mother Catherine suddenly pulled me out of the line. "Come here, Ann-Marie," she said. That was the only time she called me that. They never used our Christian names and if ever they did you could see a child getting all excited – it did so lift us to be called by our names. . . anyway, on this occasion Mother Catherine took me into the store-room and powered me down and drummed it into me that I scratched myself on the hedge. The doctor said, "My goodness, what happened? What were you up to?" I had no intention of telling her the truth because if I did I was going to get another beating.'

The threat of being sent to the Gloucester Street laundry 'reformatory' in Dublin hung like a dark shadow over all the girls. They spoke of Therese Dwyer. 'She had brains to burn. She was so clever that it must have been frustration with her if she was difficult. She had a terrible time at the reformatory. Phil O'Brien was sent there too. She was a bit wild and she tried to run out of the orphanage at night. Diana Sweetman went as well. She had pulled off Mother Anne's head-dress when she was being hit, then she got the strap off Mother Anne and beat her down the stairs. We thought it was the greatest thing we'd ever seen.'

Ann-Marie remembered Angela Moran. 'Mother Scholastica really loved her ever since she was brought into the orphanage as a baby. She used to bring Angela up half her own dinner, and she'd give the rest of us a little something and say, "Aren't they feeding you at all?" Angela and a couple of other girls sneaked out one night.[12] They were found out and sent to the reformatory. I'd say it broke Mother Scholastica's heart.'

The 1908 Act provided for the removal, on summary conviction, to a certified reformatory school, of industrial school children over the age of twelve who had 'escaped', or who were found 'guilty of a serious and wilful breach of the rules of the school, or of inciting other inmates of the school to such a breach' or, at the order of the Minister for Education, of children 'found to be exercising an evil influence over the other children.' But transfers to Gloucester Street were illegal because it was not certified and was thus outside the provisions of the Act.

Despite the tragedy in 1943, fire drill was still not carried out regularly. Some girls could remember having drill once, others not at all. Ann-Marie said, 'We were told that if a fire started at night we were to go straight down and out a certain door. They showed us where the keys were at night. There were other exits, and there was a fire escape, but the doors were always locked and not like the ones you can bang open. Two years before I left they put in fire extinguishers. There were bolts on all our dormitory doors and they were locked on the inside so, in a fire, we could have unlocked them. The nursery with the bigger babies was locked from the outside. The younger ones were upstairs with us so that we could feed them. We never had fire drill.'

The figure of Miss O'Reilly flickered, peripherally, through their memories. The recommendations of the report had been ignored. Ann-Marie told us, 'When the nuns went on retreats she'd be left in charge of us. Even then I used to think it was a bit strange after what had happened during the fire.'

The girls remembered her as both mad and frightening. Nora said, 'She'd spend hours going round the Seven Stations of the Cross in the chapel, praying. If she saw you talking in mass she'd reach out and hit you from behind with a cane. Sometimes she'd pull you out into a side aisle and give you a real beating – it did so shame us in front of the people.'

Tina recalled, 'She used to torture herself by putting tight curlers into her hair and by soaking her feet in scalding water – she gave us sixpence to bring it up for her. And she was always going on about hell fire and the devil. "Three times the flames will come for you! And the devil will be waiting for you, and the flames will devour you!"'

Some images the girls evoked of their childhood and adolescence dominated others: the perpetual praying and scrubbing and polishing; rooting in the hen bucket for scraps of food; small, cold feet standing in the dark on marble floors; the frightened efforts to dry wet knickers and sheets; the threat of the reformatory; the constant beatings; the absence of male figures to replace fathers and brothers; the sisterly love and companionship; the loyalty to the nuns which made Cissie Meehan ask that we should tell the good as well as the bad; and, for many, a terrible sense of isolation relieved momentarily and infrequently by small acts of kindness.

But authority continued to report that all was well.

> *Department of Education Report, 1962: 'Great credit is due to managers of the schools, particularly the girls' schools, for the manner in which they strive to make the lives of the children as happy as possible during their enforced absences from home.'*

8

'The Soil of the World'

Eugene O'Brien told us, 'Once they came out, all they could do was go away. You know what it's like coming from an orphanage – they'd no manners or education. And of course they had religion dinned into them but it didn't seem to do them much good. They were very bad-mannered somehow. I've met them sometimes in the Presbytery and that, and they were very unobliging and bad-tempered. I'm surprised any of them would talk to you about it – it was a disgrace to be there. It's thought of as something shameful to have come from those places.'

Cavan bar-owner, John Kiely said, 'When the girls got out, they were wild, like animals. A fellow could do what he liked with them.'

Annual Report of the Department of Education, 1959: 'After-care of Industrial School children is exercised in many ways, particularly by finding suitable employment for them, personal visits to them, correspondence with and reports on them by social workers.'

Before Elizabeth Bright went to her first job as a domestic at the age of sixteen in 1966, Mother Catherine handed her a book on sex education and later asked her if she had understood it. 'I replied truthfully that I hadn't understood a word.' Nothing further was said to her about such matters before she left. 'One evening I went out with a young fellow. His two friends came too. The fellow I was with said to me, "Would you like a baby?" and then he did it. It was right up against a wall, perhaps that's why I didn't get pregnant, but I've always been lucky. Then I saw that the two other fellows were standing there in the shadows looking on. When I got back to the house I was bleeding and frightened. I thought I was dying and told the other girl from the convent who was working with me. She said, "God, you're pregnant!" and she told someone who told the nuns, and I was taken up to a doctor in Dublin. But I was bleeding again by then so they knew I was just menstruating. After that I knew what it was all about and told fellows

I wouldn't.'

Elizabeth had always wanted to find her mother. After years of searching she was put in touch with an official in the Department of Education who had helped many other girls in similar situations. He traced her mother and, because she refused to disclose her address, he acted as intermediary when letters passed between mother and daughter. 'When I got the first letter I couldn't read it. You can see it's the first one because it's covered with blotches from where I cried all over it. I was delighted and disappointed at the same time. Delighted because I was the only one, but disappointed because I had no brothers or sisters. My mother said she had got married when she was forty-six but had had a hard life up till then. She and her husband owned a little petrol station in the country and she was terrified that her husband would ever find out about me.' She was so frightened that eventually the correspondence ceased. 'I would love to see her, just once, and I'd never even let on who I was.'

Elizabeth married a man who beat her and for years they had very little money. Their diet, even when she was pregnant, consisted mostly of potatoes. Cheerfully she claims that 'things are better now'. Her mother's letters are tied with a ribbon, carefully wrapped and kept with her marriage certificate, her book with the orphanage girls' addresses and locks of her two babies' hair.

Connie Fitzpatrick, who had been Mother Anne's favourite and loved the orphanage, left St Joseph's at the age of eighteen in 1965 and went into domestic service. 'I missed the girls and I used to cry a lot and be frightened of people. I knew nothing about men. We learnt everything too late. We just went out that courtyard door into the world.' She left her first job because her employer made advances to her. Subsequently, she says, she has slept with many men and has been lucky to avoid pregnancy. 'I have no will power where sex is concerned. I used to get kind of depressed and drink a lot but I've stopped that now.' She has since spent some time in hospital suffering from depression and anorexia nervosa and her present whereabouts is unknown.

Margaret and Deirdre Ryan left St Joseph's in 1966 shortly before it closed. Margaret says she was asked if she would like to go and live with a Mrs Crowley with whom they had stayed during school holidays. 'But I didn't know if it was for a month or a year. Nothing was explained to me. I said I would go. Deirdre said she wouldn't. I was very lonely and cried a lot because I missed the girls. Mrs Crowley was very good to me. I couldn't say a word against her. She even bought me a record-player. I went to secondary school while I was with her. I left there after three years – I can't explain it but I didn't want to stay any longer – and I went to Booterstown where Deirdre was. It wasn't clean the way our orphanage had been but the nuns didn't hit the girls. I did my Intermediate Certificate and passed.

'I went to a live-in job working in a shop with Deirdre and then didn't she get pregnant. I was mad with her for marrying him because I knew he was no good. I had lots of jobs after that, nearly always in shops or in hotels for the summer. I'd never been told the facts of life so I never knew what to let a man do. The other girls used to sleep around and go with married men but I never could abide that. I got pregnant before I married Joe. Then he went off to England but he sent me £10 every week and when he came back we got married. I like it here in the country although I was lonely at first and wanted to run away. But it's healthy for little Tom and I like gardening: I've planted onions and parsley and potatoes. I used to wonder how I'd manage when I got married but I wash the clothes and look after the child and I always have a dinner on the table ready for when he comes in. I never hit Tom though I'd slap him the odd time. I never tell anyone where I'm from. I tell the neighbours different things to keep them quiet. I talk to Joe sometimes about Cavan and the things that happened. I don't go to mass but sometimes in the afternoons when I take Tom for a walk we go into the church and I say a prayer.'

She worries constantly about Deirdre who has not been so lucky. 'I'm different from Deirdre, aren't I? I wish she wouldn't go back to that fellow but I think she likes being abused. She likes to get sympathy. I used to lie awake at night crying about her.'

Deirdre was quiet and withdrawn when we met her. She was very thin and pale, as was her four-year-old child. She spoke very little. The child was utterly silent. When she was sent to the industrial school at Booterstown, she says that some effort was made to teach her to read. This failed. She had a succession of jobs. 'The nuns in Booterstown went on trying to help me. They gave me food and money but after a while I stopped going to see them.' Then she became pregnant. 'I only married him to give the child a name.' She told us that her husband often gave her no money at all, and frequently beat her up. 'Once I needed five stitches in my head. I was terrified of him. We had no light or gas for six months while the baby was in hospital.' The child had had to go into hospital for massive shots of calcium: her baby diet had been tea and bread. A year later her husband had been forced to leave the flat and the marriage was annulled. Many people have tried to help her: social workers, Margaret, Nora O'Hanlon, the nuns. Recently we heard that she had gone back to her husband and was pregnant again.

Cissie Meehan was sent out to work at the age of thirteen. She, too, had many jobs. In some she was badly treated and on one occasion the nuns got to hear of it and brought her back to the orphanage. 'Then I got a job in a hospital in Dublin. I got double wages – £14 a week. I worked from seven in the morning until five as a ward maid, then until twelve at night as a kitchen maid, then I'd go dancing. Life was beginning to be a bit rosy then.'

But not for long. She met a man, fell in love and became pregnant: 'I know it was wrong but he had a lovely smile. It was only the once and we were going to get married.' But he was killed in a car crash and Cissie was sent to stay with the Good Shepherd nuns in Limerick. 'It was like a prison there. The nuns were very deceitful and lied to me about my fiancé's mother ringing up – they wouldn't let me talk to her. I never told her I was pregnant because she'd been very good to me and I had too much respect for her to give her the shame and the worry. I had the baby in St Patrick's home in Dublin. She had lovely blue eyes. It was very nice there and I kept her until she was adopted at four months.'

Cissie later met another man, became pregnant and married him. He was violent to her for some years until she hit him back. Since then they have got on quite well. When we met her, she was in a state of euphoria because, after years of searching, she had managed to trace her mother, now an invalid and living in Wales. On a tape-recording, punctuated with the sound of sobs, her mother explained that she had been compelled by desperate poverty to put Cissie – her youngest child – into St Joseph's when her husband deserted her. She had then left the country to find work.

Correctly assuming that Cissie was committed until she was sixteen, she wrote to the nuns some time before this but was told that Cissie had gone. She claimed that they had refused to give her any address. Meanwhile, Cissie herself had asked for her mother's address but was told by the nuns that they had no record of it. Mother and daughter came together through the chance intervention of a parish priest whose aid they had sought. 'I've had hard times,' Cissie said. 'But now that I've found my mother, nothing else matters.'

By chance we located the Morans, for whom Cissie had worked briefly. Mr Moran was an ex-Army officer with an air of command. Cissie, he said, was the second girl they'd had from Cavan. 'We only kept the first one four days. I was fascinated by her because she was so wild. I don't think she had ever been let outside the convent door. She was mad on anything in trousers. She was wonderful at scrubbing and polishing and, although she was a bit simple in a wilful way, she was intelligent enough to be taught. She never smiled but she wasn't intentionally rude. She was useless to us, a total liability. I thought it was a disgrace to have let her loose. We had to take her back. I remember the silence in the orphanage. I wouldn't have believed there were young children around. The rooms glistened with polish and you got the feeling that where you had been standing would be immediately re-polished when you left. It was pathetic to see her going off. She walked away with her hands together in front of her and her head down. I tell you I'd almost want you to use my name, but I have a sister a nun and it could embarrass her.

'We only had Cissie for a month or so and then we had to leave her back too.' He did not realise she was only thirteen. 'We were led to believe she was sixteen or seventeen but, mind you, she could have been that. She was good to the children and just wanted to play with them. But when she took them out she'd make dates with fellows on building sites and we had to stop it. Our children were capable of looking after her instead of the other way round. I have nothing to say against the girls. It was not their fault. It was my impression that they were beaten into submission. If you raised your voice they'd cower in a corner.' Eilis (one of the women who attended the national school in the early 1950s) told us, 'Now I am appalled to think of what happened to those girls in later life. At the time I didn't think too much about it although I dimly realised that when they left they had no homes to go to.' She remembered one girl in particular: 'She truly exuded goodness and charity. She wanted to be a nun but couldn't enter because she was illegitimate. I met her years later in Dublin working as a domestic in a hotel. It was a terrible shame because she was so bright.'

The Bishop of Kilmore, in his funeral oration for the dead orphans, had reminded the congregation that those 'dear little angels, now before God in Heaven, were taken away before the gold of their innocence had been tarnished by the soil of the world.'

We heard of so many who had illegitimate babies (often more than one); of girls who had drifted into prostitution, or who had become involved with drugs and were known to Dublin's vice squad, or who had spent time in mental hospitals. We heard about Theresa Dwyer, who had 'brains to burn', last seen wheeling a hand-cart through the streets of Dublin. When we tried to talk to her she refused to see us, saying that the nuns 'had done their best'.

In the year in which Cissie was sent out to work (1959), of the 113 jobs to which discharged girls were sent that year, 102 could only be described as domestic. A report published in 1966 by a voluntary body inquiring into industrial and reformatory schools ascribed the reason for this to the girls' low intelligence. We failed to find evidence to support this contention.

Cissie recalled, 'The awful part of those years was that there was no one to turn to. You didn't know where to go when you were in trouble. I don't blame the nuns at all, they did their best for us. But maybe if you write this book people will understand a little bit what we went through and what it was like for girls from orphanages.'

In May, 1968, a Dublin branch of the Legion of Mary (a Catholic lay organisation) produced for its members the following report on young prostitutes, aged between sixteen and twenty-four, living in the city:

> We find that the greater proportion of those involved are illegitimate orphans who have spent the greater portion of their childhood in orphanages and convents. Apart from their mental capabilities this abnormal form of life with too many mothers and sisters and having no fathers or brothers appears to have an effect which may be almost impossible to overcome.
>
> They appear to have no training but only warnings on how to behave and deal with boys and men. They appear to have received little or no training to fit them to earn a living or on the problems or economies of looking after themselves materially in a flat or hostel. In this state they are suddenly discharged into public life without a necessary, supervised transitional period and are faced with an almost inevitable future. To us the reaction seems to be so violent

that it might be said that they make straight for the first available man out of complete control.

9

'God Help The Poor Orphans, They're Not Normal'

Sally, b. 1940

When she talks about Mother Assumpta, a big smile lights up Sally Johnson's face. 'The sight of her made my day. I'd go into the laundry and she'd say, "Take the weight off your feet" and make a cup of tea. The others had no one. I always had her.'

Sally, a bright, good-natured mother of four boisterous children and wife of a solid, decent man, an accounts clerk, lives in a semi-detached house in the English midlands. She believes she was the first baby taken into the orphanage. 'They put me in a basket and left me with Assumpta in the laundry. I saw on my notes that I didn't walk until I was three. Perhaps it was the lack of space!'

She was three at the time of the fire and by then, presumably, would have been sleeping with all the babies and very young children saved from the Infirmary. 'We younger ones were put in the old sanatorium outside the town while they were rebuilding. I can remember the day they brought us back, all the nuns were lined up on the stairs and Mother Assumpta said "Where's Sally?" and picked me up and pressed a sweet into my hand. . . I can see her face as she did it.

'I went into the orphanage at fourteen months. Assumpta told me that my mother was only seventeen when I was born. Her parents chucked her out. She went to work and I was left with her landlady and she didn't feed or change me all day. I was committed till I was sixteen. My mother always wrote and sent presents and she did come to see me. I remember she kept crying. Once she asked me what we ate. We did not want people outside to know how we were treated and I told her we had tea, toast and eggs for breakfast, meat every day, a lovely dinner and as much bread as we wanted. In fact we had horrible half-cooked stirabout for breakfast and we were half-starved. I can see her crying, saying, “No, I know you don’t have that to eat. I know, I know.” I think she must have asked Assumpta.

‘When I last saw her she would have been thirty at the most, but she looked old – she was thin, wizened and had a very lined face. She must have had a very hard life. When I left the orphanage I did ask the Legion of Mary to help me find her but they said it was a risk. Anyway, they couldn’t find her. I’d like her to know that I’m okay.

‘I was always terrified of Mother Bernadette. She was only young when she came – in her twenties or thirties at the most – but she hated me because of Assumpta, I think. I remember her beating the hell out of me with a broom. I smack my children if they drive me to it, but I would never really hurt them, and certainly couldn’t lift a stick to them. I remember one beating in particular. The one I got on Christmas Day for having a hole in my jumper. The bigger ones used to kick us in the shins and grumble when we had to take them our clothes to be mended and I was frightened to go in. I had my jumper rolled up so Bernadette would not see the hole. She made me roll it back down and when she saw it she went for me. When I escaped to Assumpta she made me tea on her awful old boiler fire, and one of the other girls mended it.

‘Once we were sitting in the dining room and Bernadette hit me for some reason and I said to her, “How dare you hit me – I’ll report you to the cruelty man.” I ran for it, then, and she came after me hitting me around the head and arms and I was screaming and screeching. After she stopped I ran into the laundry. Assumpta was crying, she knew my voice and could hear me screaming. “Why do you make her so mad?” she said. “You know how cruel she is.”’

‘I used to threaten to run away but I never did. Perhaps I was lucky that I knew no different. We had grotty clothes and no coats except to go out to the cathedral for mass. I always got rubbish because Bernadette gave it out. I loved books, all I wanted to do was to read. There was a big press full of books and comics too, but all for show. We only had them out now and again. Some of the girls brought me in books from outside, sometimes from the library. Assumpta gave me the newspapers that she got from the presbytery to light the boiler and I’d sit by her fire and read. I feel resentful now at my lack of education. But I escaped the workroom and I escaped the kitchen – I didn’t mind helping Assumpta in the laundry – that was lovely. We were never allowed to study or get above our station.

'I sat the scholarship for Loretto convent – I was the only one from the orphanage. I came fifth from the county, but they only took the first three. Instead of encouraging me to study, Mother Bernadette made me go and look after the children. I remember once I was going off to do my history homework. She stopped me and said I was to go in and look after the little ones. I told her I had to do my homework, but she said, "Oh, take it in there with you." There were about a dozen toddlers to be looked after so I just gave up and shut my book.

'I went on to the Technical School later with three others. I don't think they sent anyone before or after us. We were made to do domestic science. I knew they were doing a commercial course upstairs and I wanted to do that so that I wouldn't have to be a domestic. I remember going there one day with blood-matted hair from being hit with a brush. The teacher could see there was something wrong. "What's the matter?" she asked. "I've got a cold," I told her. We didn't want people to know we were beaten. She made me sit in the front near the fire, and I saw her and another teacher giving each other a look. They knew what went on.

'There were some lovely nuns, like Mother Scholastica and Mother Paschal, God rest her. Mother John was kind – she was an English SRN. We hated the way Mother Carmel said, "You orphans·" Mother Assumpta and Mother John always said, "The children", or "Our children."

'After the tech, I worked in the convent kitchen. That was lovely, quite different. I worked at the presbytery for three months after that. There was no pay until I asked for something, but I did the shopping and could get all the food I wanted to eat. Then I went to Dublin and worked for a family who were very nice. I was a bit lazy, I always had to be told what to do and when to do it because I'd just sit there reading. It was my happiest year. I used to go to Irish dancing places and every Sunday I went to the Metropole for the tea-dances.'

Sally made friends with a girl who had been brought up in the industrial school at Booterstown, Dublin. 'She took me out there one day. I couldn't believe it. It was an entirely different style of life there. It was very happy. She just rolled in with me and made herself a cup of tea, quite at home.'

Then the family she was with went bankrupt. She returned to the convent and Mother John arranged for her to start her nurse's training

– 'You're not going out to scrub floors, girl with those brains!' – in a hospital in Kent where there was a Catholic matron. When she arrived at the hospital she found that one of the town girls who had been in the same class at the national school was also training there. 'I was so appalled I more or less ran. I didn't want it to be known that I was from the orphanage. I wanted a clean slate. I found another hospital and put down a false home address, but the nursing supervisor somehow guessed and had me in for a talk. She said that in life I would be judged on my own worth, that there was no shame whatsoever in having been brought up in an orphanage, and that her own cousin who had been reared in Dr Barnardo's home was a fine fellow.

'I've been very fortunate, really. I have good friends and my mother-in-law is like a mother to me. My husband has never let me make excuses for myself because of my childhood. "You are as you are," he says. Kay – she's the only one I kept up with from St Joseph's – competes with her child for her husband's attention, but he is very good to her. Her nerves are bad. I asked her if she would talk to you but she said she could not bear to bring it all back again.

'We went back to Cavan once to see Assumpta. It was in the early '60s. They had a TV and I thought things looked better, that they weren't being hit. Mother Bernadette had gone. I can still see the rosary beads and cane, hanging side by side from her waist as she'd give you a bang on the head with the bell in the morning. But I had Assumpta. I always had Assumpta.' And the big smile lights up her face.

Joan, b. 1946

We had heard quite a lot about Joan before we met. The other girls' stories had portrayed her as tough, the friend of the bully, Sheila Delaney, a girl the nuns were almost afraid of because she did not seem to care what they did to her. We heard that she had a baby by a 'black man'. We were not sure what our reception would be and half-anticipated some kind of squalid situation.

We found her in a block of council flats in London. Her gleamingly-clean windows were conspicuous by their whiter-than-white net curtains, the doorstep was scrubbed and the row of empty milk bottles shone like polished crystal. She had curly shining hair, a calm manner, cockney accent and a fresh 'Woman's Own' look about her. Her common-law husband was indeed black – a charming, intelligent man. They had a five-year-old son, a beautifully behaved, bright child. Joan's only concern in talking to us was that her mother, whom she had recently found, should not be identified. She could not remember what age she was – her husband reminded her that she was twenty-nine.

She said she had been put in the orphanage at the age of two and had few memories of the early years except 'Mother Bernadette was a lovely nun, but Mother Andrew, she was real cruel. She didn't care where she hit you. But I got used to being hit. While they were doing it, I'd say to myself "It's all right, Joan. Tomorrow it'll be all over." I think I got more beatings than the rest. Phil O'Brien was like me. She couldn't care less. The nuns hated her and sent her to the reformatory. She had a baby later.'

We had been told a story about Joan which we had not believed: that, after she left St Joseph's, she and another girl had gone to the convent where Mother Anne and Mother Catherine then were, and had shouted abuse at them. She remembered the incident quite clearly. 'We went to see Mother Clare – a nun who looked after us once but had no roughness in her – and we saw the two of them. We giggled and laughed at them and I shouted out, "They used to wallop us. We don't care now. They can't hit us now, can they Sheila?" I didn't hate the nuns. I just did not care. But now I often think that without them where would we have been?' We mentioned that they had received state aid. 'No! Really?' We never knew they got money for us.

'There were some lovely nuns, but there were some wicked ones as well. Mother Benedict – she was a teacher – hated me. I don't know why. "How many times did you look at yourself in the mirror?" she said to me. "Once or twice to put my hair straight," I said, and she slapped me across the face. She put two lumps of twine in my hair when the other girls would have a ribbon. Because of her I did look at myself and I said, "Not bad, you're not so bad!" The nun that took us for cookery was cross too. She couldn't see too well, and we'd take handfuls of the sugar out of the bowl and she'd sing out, "Stand up the girl who knows the girl who took the sugar." We'd take the bacon rind out of the bucket at cookery classes. My child doesn't eat out of the garbage bin, does he?'

She remembered the town girls at the national school being snobby. 'They'd say things like "My mammy says you're a bastard" but I gave it back to them.' She said she had never learned to read or write. 'I wouldn't concentrate at school and when I was twelve they sent me out to work at a doctor's house in Dundalk. There were nine children but the family were nice. I got £1 a month. I had to work hard – there wasn't such a thing as a half-day. But after I'd been there for a couple of months the nuns sent for me. It wasn't because I had done anything wrong. It was probably because the medical inspector was coming to the school and she would want to know where I was. She used to see the marks on me and she'd ask, "Who did that" and I'd tell her and she'd say, "Oh, dear, we'll have to do something about that." The other girls were so frightened they wouldn't say anything. I'd tell anyone. I sometimes think it's funny I'm so normal when I think of all that bashing around the head I got when I was small.

'I had so many different jobs and I was always so unhappy and lonely that I used to cry. I was still only a child I suppose, and I missed the girls. Work, work, work – that's all it ever was. But I liked the boys. I liked their company, for the excitement, for the kissing and cuddling. There was nothing else till I was twenty-one.'

Then she was sent to train as a children's nurse. 'I love children and I know I was good at the job. I remember the nuns sending me to confession and a priest came and said to me, "What do the boys do to you? Do they pull your knickers down?" Some of those priests were horrible. Then he said, "Do you know what I have under my habit?" I replied, in all innocence, "Yes, father, your petticoats." I was ignorant about sex. We all were and that's why we got into such trouble. If I'd had a baby and it had to be adopted I would have gone out of my mind. Lots of the girls had several babies before they married.'

Joan never finished her training. She went to work in a factory in England, met Andreas and they have been together for the last nine years. She regrets that she never became a children's nurse: 'I never seemed to get the right encouragement. I'd love a big family. I don't believe in smacking children because it doesn't do a bit of good. I know that from what was done to myself. When I got beaten I almost looked forward to it. And I knew it would be over by tomorrow.'

Before she left Ireland Joan heard that Elizabeth Bright had found her mother. Joan contacted the same official in the Department of Education and was also successful. 'My mother's married now. Her husband was very good about it when she told him. I criticised her a lot at first for what she had done to me, but she explained how she had wanted to tell him and had lain sleepless at night thinking and worrying about me, but she put off telling him from week to week and then months and years. We're good friends now, though. Very close. She lives in Ireland and I wouldn't want anything in the world to hurt her.'

We asked whether she practised her religion. 'Are you joking? The little boy is not christened. I don't believe in it, so why go? But I say to Andreas, "If I hit the bucket and you don't look after Andy I'll haunt you!" Joan now works as the cleaner in a children's nursery, doing without any effort – and very competently one may be sure – her 35 hour week in 20 hours. She has taught herself to read from her son's nursery school books.

Everything seemed fine: her mother found, a good man, a lovely child – and another, to her delight, on the way – a nice flat and a good job. She did not seem to have any friends: 'I keep myself to myself,' she said. One got the feeling that no matter what went wrong she would survive it, just as she had in the orphanage, by saying to herself, 'It'll all be over tomorrow.'

Ann-Marie, b. 1947

Other girls had told us 'Ann-Marie Hanley had no tears. She could not cry.' She thinks she must have been at least four years old when she was taken into the orphanage by her mother. 'The first thing I saw, and I can see it now, was all the children huddling in the yard where the heat comes out of the laundry in the pipe. I let go my mother's hand and I ran over to see what they were doing. When I turned around to look for her she was gone. The next thing I remember is sitting in the refectory and knowing it was these nuns who were going to be looking after me, and the most terrible feeling came over me.

'I used to cry myself to sleep every night, and I was slapped for it, so I had to stop – you do, after you get a hiding. The others had been there since they were babies. It was worse for me because I remembered my mother. She'd always send me a birthday present. She never forgot. And I always had something at Christmas. Until I was nine. Then she came and stayed in the town for a week. She told me she was going away but she didn't say where. I never believed I wouldn't see her again but I never did and she didn't write. I have this feeling that she did care for me and that maybe she was driven away from me. Or maybe she was getting married. I still remember the last card she sent me. It had a little train on it, and you could put your finger inside and move the train around. A priest from Cavan told me that some of the mothers were ordered not to come again by the nuns, because they were bad women and they did not want them influencing the children.

'My mother had lovely auburn hair. I went for a walk with her that week. I was holding her hand and one of the town girls shot over to me and she said, "Is that your Mammy?" because I used to tell them at school that my Mammy was coming to take me away.

'My worst years were after that, when I was around nine or ten. As I got older I wanted to know where my mother was living. Mother Scholastica must have known but she was gone so old that she couldn't remember. I tried to find out from the other nuns but I couldn't. Once you were there they forgot about your parents. You were in their care.

'We used to go and look at where our relatives' addresses were locked away in a room. I can still see the writing and the address. I'd just enjoy looking at it, and at my mother's name. When I got married and our photograph was in the *Evening Press* I had this feeling that she was looking at it though when she saw the address she probably said to herself, "No, she doesn't belong to me" because a friend had let me use her address.

'Wait till I tell you an awful sad thing that happened when I was twelve. They were always mixing me up with another girl whose mother worked in the town and used to come and visit her. Well, this day, one of the nuns said that Ann-Marie Hanley was to come – her mother was in to see her. When they called me I was in the chapel – I used to go in there a lot to pray that she'd come back – and I ran down the yard, and when I got there. . . they'd made a mistake. I'll never forget it. Never forget it.

'When I was about eight they gave me a pair of boys' boots, with tabs at the back. I hated them so and cried because I didn't want to wear them. Mother Andrew tore a piece off a box they used to keep soap in and beat me across the leg and tore bits from the top of my thigh. She was a wicked woman. But the nuns had their good points, too. Mother Anne made us all slips with lace at the bottom and I remember turning up my skirt so the lace would be seen. And she got rid of our long bloomers and got us proper panties.

'But one night – I would have been about fourteen – one of the girls was burning something in the workroom fire and I was so cold I was standing over the fire and another girl said, "Look, a bird has fallen down the chimney!", and, like any child, I got the poker at it, but it wasn't a bird, but a bloody thing. It was a sanitary towel but I didn't know that then. The girl that put it in the fire went and told the nun I was poking at this thing and they got me out and murdered me. They all took turns at hitting me on the bed, two of them holding me down, one by the head and one by the feet, and I got the strap left, right and centre. . . yes, without clothes – when they beat you your clothes were pulled off and your pants pulled down. When I got up off the bed I was in desperate pain all over, but mostly in my stomach. I went to the toilet and you can imagine the fright I got when I saw all the blood. It was the first time I got my period, though I didn't get one again for some time. They beat it out of me.

'But I was rough, too. I'd kick and pull hair if I was attacked by one of the other girls. I was always in trouble and I always got blamed. I seem to have been hated by all the girls and by the nuns. I know that most mothers will smack a child sometimes. The trouble with the nuns was that they didn't know when to stop. Sometimes when they'd been beating you, you'd want to throw your arms around them and beg them to forgive you.

'They'd tell us that if we didn't behave we would be sent away to Gloucester Street, to the reformatory. When I was ten or eleven I was taken there one day by Mother Anne and another nun in a car. I was terrified out of my life that they were going to leave me there. I can see it all clearly as if it was yesterday. It reminds me of a scene in a film. All the girls had their hair chopped short like as if they were boys. I'm not joking, but they were wearing sacks – anyway, the stuff you make sacks out of. They were working so hard at the laundry that the sweat was coming down their faces and there was steam everywhere.

'Mother Anne said to me, "I don't want you to talk to Philomena O'Brien in case you disturb her" – she was one of the older girls they'd sent there – but I didn't see her anywhere, I'd say they had her locked away. We sat and had tea with the nuns and I remember them talking and saying that Phil was unsettled.

'I got my Primary Certificate when I was only nine. We got a good education really. When I was ten I had to look after eight babies. We had them in the dormitories so that we could feed them when they cried. I would be up four times in the night and I used to be so tired I couldn't do my homework. I was to continue into the secondary school but I had an accident, climbing up to get a tennis ball on a low roof. I fell off and broke my arm. We had been playing in a part of the yard where we weren't supposed to go and they told me I wouldn't be allowed go on with school because of my disobedience. I was put in the kitchen for about six weeks, then a nun came who knew shorthand so they decided to let a few of us do a commercial course in the secondary school. We did Pitman's and I got my first exam but then that nun went and another came who could only do Gregg's and got us confused so I was taken out of school again and put into the kitchen. We'd often be taken out of school for a while to do a job until someone else became available.

'There is something I am still ashamed of. I was twelve or thirteen when I was taken off the commercial course to look after five tinker children. They used to dirty themselves and it was my job to clean them. I used to thump the oldest, a boy, aged five or six because he used to dirty his pants. He was frightened of me, I know.

'I left the orphanage when I was fifteen. I was sent to work for titled people, first for £1 and then £1 10*s.* a week as a kitchen-parlourmaid. I served at table too and had different uniforms and a cap just like *Upstairs, Downstairs*. I was only allowed out for mass – you never saw such an upright life!

'I had an awful lot of jobs after that. I worked for a cousin of the Abbess who sent her money for me to go to a commercial course twice a week. But the cousin wouldn't let me go because she wanted me to baby-sit. When I met the Abbess later she said she was disappointed in me, but I couldn't tell her that I hadn't been allowed to go. I was very lonely most of the time. I never ate with any of the families – I wouldn't have felt it was right for me, even if they'd asked me – and I mostly had to use the outdoor toilet. I wasn't allowed to wash in the bathroom so I used the kitchen sink.

'I met Dermot at a dance when I was sixteen. We'd only been going out for two or three weeks when he invited me home and from then on his mother was wonderful to me. We got engaged but I'd say to myself, "I don't want to get married, I don't want to settle down." I could never have any kind of sensible conversation with Dermot because I was so ignorant and so I'd make sure I'd never say too much. I was afraid I'd make a fool of myself. I used to feel sick with tension. I now realise the nuns shouldn't be given the care of children, but I'm glad I was brought up that way rather than somewhere where the father would be cruel to the children when he had too much to drink.

'When Dermot was drinking, after we got married, I used to lie awake crying, thinking that bad and all as the convent had been it was better than this. I used to get up in the morning to change the children, then I'd give them a bottle and I'd take a pill and go back to sleep. I used to wish that I could wake up and find myself back in the orphanage with all the girls around me again.'

Ann-Marie was twenty-seven when we met, though we had to work it out. Like several of the girls she could not recall her age off-hand. A subdued, attractive girl, she was wearing jeans and a sweater and no make-up. She has four children. Her husband, a skilled mechanic, is an intense, emotional man. They have been married for ten years and live in a new housing estate. She told us most of her story in one long session. Her husband was present most of the time, and we gradually realised that she had never before talked to him about life in the orphanage. We wondered why this was. She replied that he had never really asked her. He said that there was an orphanage in the town he had been brought up in, and people spoke about the boys as though they were sub-human. 'You didn't say that someone was an orphan, you said someone was "only" an orphan. I couldn't understand a lot of her ways in the beginning or how she could be so ignorant – incapable of holding any kind of conversation. For example, she had never heard of Hitler. But in Ireland, where the church was concerned, you did not question anything.'

Ann-Marie said later that, after our long talk, she was physically sick for two days.

She presents to the world a picture of confidence and competence. She is a good housekeeper and a loving mother. She looks after the family finances. When she went out to work again recently – doing domestic work – she negotiated wages well over the local rates. Her employer described her as 'well-trained'. She was also teaching herself to type. She had lived on the estate for three years. She said she had had previous experiences where neighbours who learned of her origins looked down on her. One of her worries was what would become of her children if she died.

A year or so before we met she had chanced to meet Mother Catherine. 'She had gone so thin she was almost unrecognisable. She seemed pleased to see me although I was abrupt with her. I don't believe it occurred to her that I could have remembered what she had done to me. Maybe she had even forgotten herself. I think that when they went back to the ordinary life of a nun, they must have started to think about the things they had done.'

The last time we saw Ann-Marie was in the evening. Her husband was away overnight. We went into the hall and she reached up to the top of each door, took down a key and locked each one, in turn. She saw our amazement. 'Habit, I suppose,' she said.

Tina, b. 1951

We first spoke to her on the telephone nearly a year before we met. She said that she would talk to us but could not do so for a few weeks because she had exams. We waited until the date she had suggested and telephoned again. A friend told us she had gone on holiday. We tried another couple of times. The friend said she was on sick leave and, finally, that she had left. We wrote, but received no reply. Then we heard that she was working in Cork, but, worried that perhaps we had been harrassing her and that she really did not want to talk to us, we asked another girl to sound her out again. Tina sent a message that, yes, she did want to meet us. We offered to come to Cork but she said she would come to Dublin and, rather to our surprise, she telephoned a few days later and arranged a meeting. She hitch-hiked up and we spent the day together.

She was a handsome young woman, tall with smooth, dark hair and rosy cheeks. She emanated an air of solidity and dependability and seemed highly intelligent. 'I'll tell you everything,' she said.

'I have a very bad memory. I can remember nothing before I was eight. So long as I had music and books I was all right. I was in my own world. We made up lovely stories about ourselves. We all invented things about our parents.

'My mother was sixteen when I was born. I was put into St Joseph's when I was seven months old, and she went off to England, got a job and married a man she met there. Daddy is a kind, decent man. He told me he wanted Mummy to get me over but she wouldn't. She was ashamed because I was illegitimate and she had joined the Legion of Mary and had made friends. I'd seen her in the summer after they started to take me home for the holidays. I'd asked if I could come when I was eight. I didn't know she was my mother at first – I thought my auntie was my mother. Another aunt let it out when I was about nine. It meant nothing to me but after that I didn't know what to write to them in letters – "Dear Mummy and Daddy" or what. Sometimes she introduced me as her sister, sometimes as her niece. She feels guilty about me – not for putting me in the orphanage, but because I am illegitimate. It does hurt me, but I don't let her know.

'My memories of the convent are hazy. I always seem to make excuses for the nuns. They went into the novitiate and then they were thrown into a zoo – there was no thinking behind who they sent in to look after us. We were wild because of the way we were reared. I'd say we would have driven anyone mad – all kinds of children, all different ages. Mother Anne would be up till all hours making bedspreads, curtains, dresses. She fought and worked for our physical comforts but she forgot the main thing we needed. It was hopeless I suppose. We were love-starved. They thought the only way they could control us was with the strap. We used to talk in the dormitory at night and Anne once heard us and made fifteen or sixteen of us stand in the corridor just in our nighties. She went to bed and forgot about us, so we took pillows and blankets and lay in the corridor. It was quite fun.

'She walloped us next day – though I have no memories of ever being beaten. I just can't remember... but once... I was still in the little ones' dormitory, I was seen by one of the nuns talking to Maureen Harty and Joan Thomas. They would have been about thirteen. "I had expected better of you," she said. I just had on a nightie... and the strap was as thick as this... and I was trying to get away from her... I tried to hide under the bed...

'I remember things leading up to incidents, but cannot remember the actual beating. I remember the planned punishments – sixteen girls all lined up, then put over Anne's knee, with our bare bottoms. I was eleven before I realised it wasn't the way to treat children. Now I can't bear to be hit, and I literally, physically, have to hold myself back if I see anyone using physical violence. I can't bear it.

'We needed someone to relate to and we only had each other. We'd yell abuse at one another – things like "Your mother was a tramp!" Sometimes the relationships were warped – I suppose society would not think it right for the girls to cuddle each other. We just didn't know how to behave. Joan Thomas tried to get me into her bed, but I didn't fancy it. We would be looking for something from each other that we didn't have to give.

'Frances Devaney was my best friend. She was the same age and we had most in common. She had a beautiful voice – such a pity it wasn't trained. She and I and Nora O'Hanlon were the only ones sent on to the secondary school. Mother Ruth once picked Frances and myself out in front of everyone and said, "You two are filthy dirty. . . a pity you wouldn't wash yourselves!" That would have been after we had been up to do the breakfasts and clean the place and go to mass before we could straighten ourselves and go to school.

'Another time Mother Ruth said to me, "Do you ever play with yourself? Do you masturbate?" I said I did though I didn't understand for years what she meant. She told me to tell the priest in confession that I masturbated. He said, "What age are you child?" and laughed at me. Mother Ruth told me later that she gave me a hard time as a child because she wanted to make a genius out of me.

'I loved Mary Joseph, the Abbess. We both had a great love of music. "Nothing ventured, nothing gained, Tina!" she'd say. Another time she told me, "Don't worry – if they throw us out, we'll manage. You'll play the violin and I'll pass the hat!" Frances and Maureen Harty and myself used to race up to be first to get the violins to practise.

'I never studied for exams. The teachers encouraged me but the nuns never cared if you had done your homework, only if you had done your cleaning. Frances and I were the two oldest then. We'd get home from the school, have two slices of bread and marge, then there would be so many sheets and pillowcases to wash every day. Monday, say, we'd do undies, Tuesday sweaters, Wednesday dresses and so on. It all had to be done by hand. We washed and swept the classrooms and lavatories, washed, swept and waxed the halls till they shone – you could have eaten your dinner off the floor. Before school we had to clean part of the orphanage as well. That would have been from eleven until we were sixteen. We spent all day Saturday cleaning. Once a month the nuns had to go on retreat and then Frances and I had to make sure there was complete silence, yes, the toddlers and the little ones too.

'Father O'Toole – he was a friar – used to give the secondary school retreat. If any of us talked to him we used to be punished, and made to stand in the corridor. Once he stood me between his legs and rubbed me up and down and asked me didn't I have knickers on.'

When Tina left St Joseph's she decided to become a nun. She joined another order, spent a year in a convent in England, then did a year's course in theology at a seminary and was sent to teach at a private boarding school for wealthy Catholic children. 'It wasn't what I had in mind. I had a notion that if I got into an orphanage I could look after children. Anyway I left and my mother was very upset about it.' She went to Cork and got a job as a shop assistant – 'I didn't want to be a burden on anyone' – and studied for the extra subject in her Leaving Certificate which would be required to do an external degree in social science. She did the degree and is now qualified.

Later that day Tina told us why she had not followed up our first contact with her although we had not asked her. It was as we had suspected: she was going to have a baby. She fought back her tears but insisted on telling us what had happened. 'I went to a home for unmarried mothers. It wasn't too bad because my friend from work used to come to see me.' She had loved the father of the baby, and he had loved her. He had wanted to marry her before she became pregnant, and was distraught when she refused and insisted on giving the baby up for adoption. His mother, too, was fond of her and tried to persuade her to marry him. Tina could not explain to us why, although she wanted to marry him, she could not. She said she had completely broken off with him, although he was still trying to get her back.

That evening, driving her on to the Cork road, and considerably shaken by our meeting – as we were with many of the girls – we, too, tried to persuade her to go back to him, but she was adamant. She was sending her mother £25 a month for her stepsisters and brothers so that they should 'want for nothing'. She seemed so solid, so strong, so dependable. 'But,' she said, 'you're wrong, there's nothing there.' We left her, standing alone, thumbing a lift.

Martha, b. 1947

Her house is almost aggressively clean. Everything shines, including her beautiful, passionately attended babies, and crumbs are whisked off the table before they can settle. She lives in a new housing estate outside Dublin. She is convinced that there is much child neglect in the area.

The first time we met Martha was with Ann-Marie Hanley, when we asked if she would talk to us about St Joseph's. She immediately launched into the following story, and repeated it virtually verbatim when we returned for the interview some weeks later.

'The worst thing that ever happened to me in my life was the caning I got when I was eight or nine. Some of the big girls – I can't remember all their names but Diana Sweetman was one – put me up to steal out of the Black Baby box in the school. They threatened my life if I told on them. They got me to go through the window and I must have been seen by someone. The nuns took me out of bed at 12.30 at night and tried to make me tell who else was in it with me. I couldn't tell because the other girls had said they would kill me. I'll never forget that beating. All I could see was the strap flashing past me.' She was on the verge of tears as she spoke. 'I was black and blue all over. I still wake with awful nightmares of that strap and everything flashing red in front of my eyes.' She put up her hand as though to ward off a blow. 'Of all the beatings that was the worst. It's the beatings, the beatings that give me the nightmares.' She moved away and, with her back turned, she fiercely pushed a cloth around an impeccable surface.

Martha went to Cavan when she was two months old from Stamullen, the baby home run by the Poor Clares, where she had been left by her father after her mother had died at her birth. She has a faint memory that her father came to see her once to take her away and that she would not go. She would not make any effort to trace him because 'he left me'. She says that she has had visions of her mother, shining, in a white dress. She has a strong personal faith, and says she could not have survived without it.

'I was a very lonely child. I felt I was left out of everything. I wet the bed because I was terrified to get out at night and because I think I had weak kidneys. I was more in bed than at school. They'd send you to bed for the day without food as a punishment. I was never at school for a full year and when I was nine or ten I was taken out of school to work. I had to light the furnace fire, clean out the Aga cooker in the orphanage kitchen and get the water on for the cocoa for breakfast before mass. I had to scrub sixteen flights of stairs and three corridors. If I didn't do it properly, I had to do it again.

'They used to threaten to send me to the reformatory but I think I escaped that because the Mother Abbess wouldn't allow it. I was bold I know, but I suppose I was just crying out for affection. Many brushes were broken on my back.' Two other girls had previously spoken of an incident when Martha refused to be beaten when they were all getting a whacking. They described how she had turned on Mother Anne, and torn off her veil, and was then left alone. 'I was just fed up looking at leather straps and rods and it was so unfair because I'd had a beating the night before. Once I broke my ankle jumping down the stairs to get away from them before I could be beaten.

'When I was twelve or thirteen they sent me to an old couple in Ballyjamesduff. Their children were grown and gone. They were very hard on me and I was very lonely. I had to feed the fowl and plant potatoes. The old woman was nice enough but it was the man – he tried to take advantage of me. He started fiddling with me. It frightened me and it wasn't till I met my husband that I could bear a man to touch me at all – I still can't bear any other man even to put an arm around me. I could not sleep because I was frightened he would come into my room – he slept in the next room and she slept downstairs. Then one evening she came into the kitchen and found him interfering with me. She told the nuns I was carrying on with her husband so they brought me back and flogged me. They kept saying, "You were letting that man feel you," and I didn't understand what it was all about.'

Martha said she was very unsettled at the convent after she returned and, in 1962, aged fourteen, she went to work in a Dominican convent in Dublin. She was given stockings, a new skirt, jumper, coat, a towel, a bar of soap and her bus fare. 'As I was going they said, "You'll be the first one back here in trouble. Now don't allow a fellow to put a hand on your knee or go into a hayshed with a man."

'They paid me 30*s*. a week at the Dominicans and I had to work very hard. I had a half day off a week. They were strict but I had good food. I could go out but I had to be in by ten o'clock. I was very lonely. Once I was phoned by Maureen Harty and Joan Thomas. They said did I want to go to Bray for a picnic. I asked permission and I was allowed. We went into an amusement arcade with slot machines and they laughed at me when I asked about the picnic. There were fellows in there and one tried to pick me up. I said I wasn't an easy pick-up and he said, "You must be the only orphanage girl who isn't."'

She told a young nun at the Dominicans who had befriended her what had happened and she asked Martha whether she knew the facts of life. 'Of course I didn't, so then she explained most things to me, except some things she said I would learn when I was married. She warned me to be careful of men who would use me, so I made sure that I would never be used as I grew older.' This nun also helped Martha to read and write – 'I could not even write my own name when I came. I stayed in that convent for eighteen months but the nun said I should leave because I would get nowhere if I stayed with the nuns. She said I would meet a man some day when I was about twenty-four and he would be right for me.'

And so Martha did, but she met with a lot of resentment from her father-in-law who wanted them to break it off when he heard she was from an orphanage, and ignored her at the wedding. He now accords her a grudging respect. Her husband is a quiet, gentle man whom she treats with the same fierce adoration that she gives her babies. She is equally loyal to the few friends from St Joseph's with whom she still keeps in touch. They say she would do anything for them. The only things she will not tolerate are for anyone to 'use' her, and dirt.

Mary, b. 1950

She is small, with a neat figure, regular features, brown curling hair, and an open smiling expression – just like she is in the photographs taken in the orphanage. 'What a happy, cuddly child that one is!' people say when you show them. 'It doesn't look as if there was anything wrong with her.' She chain-smokes and her nails are bitten to the quick.

'I think I was four weeks old when I went to the orphanage. My mother had nine children before she was married. I was the only one she gave away. I'll never forgive her for that. People have said to me there must be a reason why she did it. I can't think of one. I'll always remember one of the nuns in the laundry room one day shouting at us that if our mothers had wanted us, there wouldn't be none of us there.

'My mother came to claim me when I was fourteen. I had never seen her or heard from her. I suppose she thought I'd be fit for work and bring in a bit of money. The nun said, "Here's your mother, go and get ready to go with her." I remember she was holding out to me a bag of pink jelly biscuits and I just snatched the bag out of her hand and ran away up the stairs with the nuns after me. I wouldn't come down and I wouldn't go with her. I did see her again, just once. I went to stay with her but I ran away after two days. It was a terrible house with no toilet or anything and the man she married drank. She's living somewhere near Dublin now but I don't want ever to see her again. Why should I?

'The nuns treated us according to our background. I got treated the worst because of my mother having all those children and because she was poor. The nuns picked on me a lot. They said I'd the devil in me.

'The children in the national school didn't talk to us much. We were always ashamed of our shabby clothes. The nuns used to call us by our surnames. I knew we weren't like other children but I never understood why. I remember sitting in school and looking at the town children and wondering *why* we were different.

'They'd clobber you for anything. They'd use a big black strap and sometimes we used to steal it and hide it down the hose-pipe in the garden so then they'd send us out to fetch a branch of a tree. They'd always take our clothes off to beat us. Sometimes just our pants, other times all our clothes and they would stand and stare at us. It used to make me feel funny.

'I never knew when my birthday was until I was seven. One of the older girls was very fond of me and she sent me this beautiful big doll with blonde hair and a pink dress. I'd never seen anything like it. Mother Catherine came up to me and said, "That's far too good for the likes of you to play with." She took it away and I never saw it again. The nuns hated us having friends. They used to watch in case we held hands or went round in two's.

'Mother Catherine and Mother Anne used to fight something dreadful. Mother Anne loved brushing our hair. Mine was long and thick and she used to make it look ever so nice. Then one day they had a fierce row and Catherine said, "McNeill, come here!" and she cut all my hair off. There was murder over it.

'When I was ten or eleven I was sent out to work. I was never much good at school – I can read a little and write my name but that's all. I worked for a man who lived near the orphanage. I got up at 7 a.m. and walked to the house. I was left back in the car at seven in the evening. They paid me half-a-crown a week which I handed over to the nuns. I had to work ever so hard. I remember being told to wash up the first morning. We only had plastic cups in the orphanage so I threw everything into the sink like I was used to. I had never seen a china cup in my life. Everything broke and the woman was mad. She hit me on the back with a brush and said she'd tell the nuns. Which she did. Then they beat me. I used to eat in the kitchen on my own from the left-over scraps.

'They nearly let me die once. I had this pain which went on for weeks and they wouldn't listen to me. They told me to get up and get out to work and I had to lift this big, heavy baby, and me nearly fainting with the pain. I got so bad that Nora O'Hanlon who was sick in the next bed rushed down to the nuns and begged them to get a doctor. I was operated on within a hour for a burst appendix.

'I worked in the orphanage for a bit before I left. I used to look after the babies. We used to be very sentimental when they were adopted and cry as we dressed them in their clothes for the last time. All the girls from Cavan cry easily.

'I got my periods when I was fourteen. I couldn't think what was happening so I told one of the other girls at a time when we were supposed to be silent. The nun caught me talking and made me stand in the corridor all day as a punishnent. Next day I had to go to her because my sheets were all stained and she hit me across the face and said why hadn't I gone to her the day before. I said I couldn't because she had punished me. She handed me out a sanitary towel and a belt and hit me again. "That'll teach you not to be so stupid."

'Mother Anne and Mother Catherine left the orphanage before I did and they kissed us goodbye. The first time in their lives. I turned my face away and wouldn't kiss them. I hated the ground they walked on. When I left, the nuns sent me to Skerries, to a farmer's family in a tiny cottage. I got ten bob a week but I hated it and used to cry every day. I saved and saved until I had £15 and then I went to England. I was happy there and people were good to me. I remember one family where the mother used to kiss me goodnight. I hated her doing it. I hated anyone touching me. I couldn't feel any affection for them and yet I knew they liked me.

'One day I just walked out. I've had so many jobs. Always domestic work. I've stayed a week in some, maybe six months, maybe one day. I couldn't seem to settle anywhere. Then I met this Italian fellow and went with him to Italy and I worked there for two years with a professor's family. I really liked that chap. He was good to me and didn't take advantage of me and explained things to me before he slept with me. The first time I nearly died, I thought it was so awful but after that I kind of got used to it. His mother came between us in the end – I suppose she thought I wasn't good enough for him.

'I came back to Ireland two years ago. I knew it was wrong to come back because I knew the awful things that had been happening to all the Cavan girls. I can't explain it. I felt it had to happen to me as well and then we would all be equal. Everything went wrong for me. I started to drink and one night some fellow put acid in my drink and I kind of attacked him. I was put in prison and a doctor came to see me and the next day in court the judge said it was the fellow should be convicted and not me.

'I've been in St Brendan's mental hospital twice. It was the doctors in there who really helped me. I stopped feeling different from everyone else. I could talk to them about things that I'd had inside me for years and they explained things to me. I've tried to kill myself three times. Always when I'd been drinking. I couldn't see the point in living any more. I was all by myself and nobody cared about me. The only people who came and visited me in hospital were the Samaritans. It's terrible when you meet someone and they say, "Where are you from? Where's your family?" and you have no-one. Maybe all the bad things are over now. I know that if I hadn't gone to Cavan I'd have been a nicer person. Some of the other girls have had terrible lives and one illegitimate baby after the other. I suppose I was lucky not to get caught but I'm terrified I won't be able to have a baby.'

During one of her stays in hospital, after a suicide attempt, Mary had an IQ test and was assessed at 112. Social workers, encouraged by her obvious intelligence, willing manner and optimistic attitude arranged for her to attend adult literacy courses. She agreed to go, but then never turned up. While in the hospital she got into a hysterical panic for no apparent reason. The cause was found to be the entrance into her ward of a visiting nun.

She is constantly washing and tidying herself. 'I'm very clean, aren't I?' she keeps saying. 'I like to have a bath twice a day. I don't want to marry,' she told us. 'I wouldn't want a man making my sheets dirty.'

When she isn't in hospital (which she never wants to leave), she always works – sometimes in a factory, but usually as a domestic in a hotel or as a mother's help. She moves from place to place, job to job. She is consistently optimistic, always hoping that things will get better for her, that she will have a boyfriend who will understand, that she will make a fresh start. People try to help her, but to no avail. With her gleeful laughter, politeness and wholesome expression, she doesn't look as though there is anything at all wrong with her. And she is always so clean.

Frances, b. 1950

We met Frances just after the birth of her third illegitimate child. She had been persuaded to keep him and not to have him adopted like her two other children. She was a gentle and intelligent person, bewildered by the events of her own life. She was lonely and had few friends, except girls from the orphanage whom she met occasionally. She was very apprehensive about her decision to keep the little boy but she hoped that it might prove she was some good after all, when her childhood experiences had taught her to think she was worth nothing.

She talked freely about the orphanage. She did so almost compulsively, smoking heavily. Sometimes after we had talked for a long time she would have nightmares. 'I want to get it right for you,' she would say, 'I don't want to tell you anything that didn't happen.

'I went to the orphanage when I was four. I didn't know my birthday until I was confirmed, then I used to figure out that I was a year older every Christmas.' She can remember little of the early years except that she got into trouble a lot. 'The nuns didn't like us having special friends or holding hands. If we were seen by Mother Catherine she'd say, "Your bodies are the Temple of the Holy Ghost. They are sacred and shouldn't be touched." I suppose we were a bit wild, but sure we didn't know any better. I had a terrible temper and I bit another girl on the wrist once and she bled like anything. And when one of them made faces at me through the pantry window I just put my fist through the pane of glass and all the bits went into her mouth. Some of us used to tell tales and suck up to the nuns, but we had a sort of loyalty amongst ourselves.

'I remember the way the town girls treated us. They used to dance round us singing, "God help the poor orphans, they're not normal". But sometimes they would ask us to their houses for tea. You'd call it entertaining the under-privileged I suppose, though I didn't think that then. I went once or twice. We sang and danced for them. But the nuns made so little of me all the time, except for my singing. Nora O'Hanlon and me, we both had nice voices and something should have been done with them. We were always made to sing if visitors came.

'When babies came into the orphanage the older girls had to look after them. When the twins came I must have been about fifteen. They were four days old and they were given to me to mind. I wasn't told what to do, I just seemed to know by instinct or perhaps by watching the other girls. At night I had them by my bed and there were times when I could have killed them because I was up so often during the night and I had to go to school the next day. One night another girl fed them instead of me. She didn't pin down the sheets the way I used to and the next morning one of them was dead. I suppose it must have suffocated. The other baby was taken away – by the mother, I suppose, though I never knew. The death was never mentioned again.

'Bernadette was brought into the orphanage when she was two. She was a gipsy and I just loved her the minute I saw her. She was so poor and desperate looking, I think she reminded me of myself. One summer the nuns sent me to work in a shop and I must have earned about £1 a week. I bought Bernadette a yellow jersey with fluff on the inside and a little blue checked pinafore and a ribbon for her hair and a pair of ankle socks. I spent my whole wages on her. She wore the clothes on Christmas Day and I never saw them again. Anything good we were given was always taken away. We never knew where it went.

'She slept in a partition next to my bed and in the night she used to knock on it and call "Francie", and I'd get up and go down this long corridor and bring her to the toilet. She was terrified of wetting her bed. Poor little Bernadette. My little darling, I adored her. I never loved anyone the way I did her, not even my own children. Her eyes were all twisted and she should have been given exercises. When I was working in Dublin I heard she was in hospital having an eye operation, and I went to see her. She stared and stared at me and then she said my name.

I was so pleased. I haven't seen her for years and anyway she wouldn't remember me. I sometimes wonder would I be a good person for her to know after everything that's happened to me.

'The other little ones used to call me "Mother" and run to me for help with their homework, especially after I started at the secondary school – I was allowed to go on there after I got my Primary Certificate. I'll never know why they let me unless it was so that they could get me to clean the whole bloody place for them. In the last year, Mother Frances Xavier and I cleaned the school together on Saturday afternoons. I'd have dropped dead for her. She was the only nun ever took an interest in me. We'd polish all the floors and clean out the bathrooms. I had to empty all the sanitary bins into newspapers and carry them down to the furnace and burn them. I hated that.

'Mother Frances used to talk to me about her life before she came to the convent. Those were my hours of happiness. I loved watching her and being with her, she was so beautiful. Once she told me about a man who had come up to her in a bicycle shed and had tried to take off her bra. I used to seek her out and look for ways to be alone with her and then I would tell her stories about fellows kissing me. I'd invent them of course but it used to excite me being able to tell them. Once I remember after I'd told her a story she said, "And did he pull down your pants? Maybe you're pregnant." I didn't even know what being pregnant meant, and I was fifteen at the time! I remember her saying, "Do you want to kiss me?" I did like her, but I didn't want to kiss her.

I hated Secondary School because I never had the right things. The girls used to laugh at me because I didn't wear a bra. Cookery classes were awful because the teacher would tell us to bring in things like half a pound of mince. Where would I have got that? And the books. All the girls could buy theirs, but I had to go to Mother Ruth and once she said, "Remember you're not paying for these." I felt so ashamed.

'There was a fancy dress party on at the school one Christmas and I asked Mother Catherine what could I go as. "Why not a scarecrow?" she said. So I asked her for some clothes and she laughed at me and said, "Go as you are!" and I went to the party in my uniform with "Scarecrow" written across my back.

'Father O'Toole used to come to the secondary school to give us a retreat and he gave us a form to fill in saying "Are you dated?" I had to ask Joan Thomas what it meant. Then he said he wanted to talk to all the girls privately. I don't know how Anne and Catherine got to hear about it, but they got a group of us into a room and they said to me, "What do you want to talk to that priest about?" and they banged my head against the wall till I thought they'd fracture my skull. I just cried and cried because I didn't know why the priest wanted us. When I did get to see him I was shaking like a leaf and he said – I'll never forget it – "Do you desire to take off my habit? I'll turn round while you get ready. Are you wearing one of those corsets?" I can't remember any more because I was crying so much. Looking back now I think he was just testing me because of what Mother Frances had told him about me being attracted to her. I much preferred women at that time even though we all thought Father O'Toole was lovely and we cried when he was moved to another parish. He had tears in his eyes at the last mass. I sometimes think he knew how we were treated.

'Other people knew, too. The nuns had beaten Tina Martin terribly on the legs once – she used to get it a lot – and she came into school all black and blue, and the teacher said, "Tina, what happened to you?" and she said, "I fell over a chair, Miss." The teacher knew well she'd been hit but nobody would ever say anything to the nuns. They were bad, bad women when I think of it now. They ruined all our lives.

'I remember some priest coming to give a lecture to them and we were forbidden to go out in the yard in case we got a glimpse of him. But I went out and of course someone told on me and Mother Catherine got a branch off a tree and beat me till white lumps came up. One of the girls was beaten black and blue for chewing the Communion bread instead of swallowing it. Why did they hit us so much? It seemed to be for such little things. Catherine was the worst. She had real tight lips and every time she came back from holidays she'd have a big boil at the end of her nose. Once in secondary school I lost my knitting needles. Actually someone had nicked them – we were always nicking things on each other – and I was told to go back to the orphanage and find them. I was wandering round not knowing what to do when Catherine found me. "Go upstairs into the shoe room!" she said, "and take off your clothes." When she came up she just sat on a little box and stared at me naked and I stood there holding myself. In the end she beat me. Would you believe she did a Child Care course somewhere after she left Cavan?

'I remember Mother Anne and Mother Catherine telling me the facts of life.

"Say the Hail Mary."

"Hail Mary Full of Grace, blessed art thou among women and blessed is the fruit of thy womb. . ."

"Stop there. Do you know what womb means?"

"No, Mother."

"Do you know where babies come from?"

"No, mother."

"Do you know that part of the body where the man goes to the toilet?"

"Yes, Mother."

"Do you know that part of the body where the woman goes to the toilet?"

"Yes, Mother."

"Well, when those are joined together that's what makes a baby and if a man ever puts his hand on your leg slap him across the face. Now you may go."

'I passed my Intermediate Certificate and I think the nuns were pleased though they didn't say so. Then one day Mother Ruth came in when a whole crowd of us were talking in class and of course big mouth me was the only one to own up. "Get out of here," she said. "Get out and don't let me see your face again." That was the end of my education. She asked me to go back later but I was stubborn and I wouldn't. I expect she only wanted me because she'd have nobody to clean the school.'

Two weeks later the nuns sent for her and told her she was going to work in Dublin. She went into the shoe room and took a bottle of travel sickness pills off the shelf. 'I'd swallowed sixteen when Tina Martin came in and grabbed them off me. If they'd been stronger I'd have been dead. I knew I wouldn't even have a suitcase and that girls in Dublin would have lovely clothes and I didn't even have a bra. I was frightened out of my wits. The day before I went I prayed hard I wouldn't have to go.' She left the orphanage in 1967. She was given a paper bag containing a jumper and skirt and a change of underwear. The nuns kissed her goodbye.

'I went to work for a woman in Donnybrook. I had to look after eight students and anybody extra who came for bed and breakfast. I was up at 7.0 a.m. and worked till 10.0 at night. I got £1 10*s*. a week and no insurance stamp. I had one half-day which began at 3 o'clock and I never had a Sunday off. I bought a bra with my first week's wages, but I hardly went out at all. I used to sit in my room and cry because I was so lonely.

'Then I went to a doctor's family in Newry. They were quite nice but they didn't let me out much. I answered an advertisement in the paper for work in America and when the doctor's wife heard about it she rang up the nuns and they said I wasn't to go.

'I had a week's holiday in Butlins when I was with the doctor. It was so terrific I'll never forget it. I went in for a talent competition and I won it and the finals were the day after I was supposed to go back to work, and the doctor's wife wouldn't let me stay. I know I'd have won it and then maybe I'd never have had all these children.

'When I left the doctor I went to the nuns in Gormanstown. They looked after old people. I worked in the kitchen and emptied bins and carried up their meals. I loved being near the sea, though many's the time I felt like running in. I used to sit on the shore and cry. I felt there was a life outside that I wasn't part of. There was a gardener there who used to take me to this little shed and make me take all my clothes off. I never knew what he was after. I really didn't. I know it sounds daft but I just used to laugh. It never clicked that this was sex. How could I have been so stupid?

'Then I got a job for the season in Butlins as a kitchen help. I got in with all the fellows and I used to go to bed with them. I didn't like it a bit – I never have really – but I did it because I thought you had to. I've never had an affair that led to bed. I always went to bed first. The fellows wouldn't take me out or anything. They weren't even nice to me. Except for Jimmy – he was the father of my first child. He was married but he used to play table tennis with me and made me save my money. Then I started getting sick in the mornings and the supervisor sent me to the hospital. It meant nothing to me to be pregnant. I didn't understand how serious it was.'

She stayed until the end of the season. Then one of the girls from St Joseph's who was working in Newry said she could go to the convent there but when she arrived they turned her away, so she went back to

Dublin and got a job cleaning in a hospital.

'I couldn't live in so I stayed in the Legion of Mary hostel. Those were my worst days I think. It was a desperate place. We'd have to make our tea over an open fire and sit and look at all these old women. The place was full of spiders. The doors were locked at 11.0 p.m. and if I was out late I'd have to sleep in a park. Then I met this fellow who said I'd make a packet on commission selling tickets for him in the street and I could live with him and his wife. So I did that until I found it hard to stand, and then he threw me out into the streets with my case. I went to a hotel – I had £1.60 in my pocket. The next morning the bill was £1.75 and I hadn't enough. The son of the owner took me up to the room and said, "Get into that bed," and I said, "Can't you see I'm pregnant?" and he let me go.

'After that I went to Ally[13] and I was sent to stay with Mrs Flanagan. She was young and pretty and very kind. Then I went to a Mrs Roche but I nicked things from her to help another girl furnish her flat. I'd never stolen before but I didn't think she'd notice, and anyway, she had so many things. But her hushand found out and I had to go. I had a couple of jobs after that – in cafés and shops. After the baby was born Mrs Flanagan and Mrs Roche came to see me and the café owner where I worked sent me flowers. I was so thrilled that I kept them till all the petals dropped off. I had no feelings for the baby: I remember signing her away and not even realising she was my own child.

'After that I got a job in Player Wills. I've never been so happy. I loved going to work. I joined the table tennis club and the music club. I felt so normal, just like everyone else. Then I got kicked in the stomach at a dance where there was a row. I went to the doctor in the factory and I had to tell him that it hurt most when I went with men. He said he would give me the pill so that I wouldn't get pregnant. But I wouldn't take it because it was against my religion and I had this belief that I wouldn't go that far, that I wasn't *that* bad.

'Shortly after that I met a fellow and got pregnant again. The girls in the factory tried to get me to stay on but I wouldn't. I was kind of ashamed that I'd messed up my chances in the one place I'd been so happy. I stayed in the flat all during the pregnancy. I was getting the dole, the rent was small and I had help from the Vincent de Paul. There were other girls in the house and the Legion of Mary came to see me twice a week. I had the telly. It wasn't too bad.

'Little Bernadette was born two days after Christmas. She'd be nine now. Just imagine. I cried for six weeks afterwards. I hated parting with her and my nerves went all to bits. I got a job in another factory which I liked and then one night Mary McNeill arrived up in my flat with her baggage and this fellow who sang in a group. She had nowhere to go so I took her in. She was desperate really, she'd be in the bed with him going hard at it, and in the end I took him off her and got into bed with him myself. I liked him in a way because he was so good-looking, but I knew well he thought nothing of me. He never took me out, he never even bought me a drink. I didn't enjoy going to bed with him, but it was the only thing brought me any comfort. I think it was the same for Mary and for all of us from Cavan.

'He was the father of my third child. I had to leave the factory because I wasn't well and I had no money to pay the rent. I went to stay with a woman who did a lot of voluntary social work. She persuaded me to keep Patrick. I'd no intention of keeping him – why would I when I'd already given away two? But she was very kind to me and she made it all sound so easy.

'If I hadn't kept the child I'd have been all right. I could have gone off somewhere, found a decent job in a factory and made a go of things. It was the worst decision of my life. People tell you to keep your baby – I'd have a thing or two to say to them if I had the nerve. They don't tell you about the loneliness of it, night after night, and the worry you have about everything. I thought keeping Patrick would stop me being bad, but it hasn't, and what is he going to think of me when he grows up? I worry all the time, about money, a flat, security. I lie awake at night thinking that if only I had something to give Patrick then maybe he wouldn't think too badly of me.

'I know I'm not pretty but the only men that like me and don't make little of me are the married ones. If I go out with John he's not ashamed to be seen with me, and he's a doctor. He'll take me to a hotel or pub and buy me a few drinks first. I'd like to be married and have a normal life. I'd love the security for me and Patrick.

'I still haven't realised that he is part of me and that I matter to him. I'm not a good mother. How can I be when I get into bed with men?' He woke up one morning when a fellow was getting dressed. "Is that my Daddy?" he said. The times I've thought of giving him up. He could be adopted or go into a Home. If I did that, do you know what would happen? My chapter in your book would end and his would begin. The girls from Cavan are all the same. We're warped. We never learn. We never, never learn.'

Three years later Frances answered a knock on her door. Standing there was one of her brothers whom she had not seen for twenty years. He had come from England to trace her. He had spent his childhood in Artane and had tried desperately to keep in touch with his brothers and sisters. He wrote a number of times to Frances in Cavan and bought the stamps with money he got from stealing eggs on the farm. She never received these letters: outside contact with relatives was always discouraged.

And then, in November 1981, an article appeared in a Dublin newspaper about a woman who was trying to contact the nine children she had abandoned when she ran away to England to escape her violent husband. She had re-married but had never told her second husband about her past. Now that she was widowed, she felt free to find her children. She had talked to her parish priest about it and he suggested she should start her search by talking to a reporter from an Irish newspaper.

Frances was one of the nine children. The next morning she rushed into the newspaper office to find the reporter who had written the story. He had her mother's telephone number in England. 'Why don't you ring her now?' he said. She picked up the telephone, dialled the number and spoke to the mother she had not heard from nor seen for thirty years. Her mother's voice was choked with tears. She wanted to come home, she said. She wanted to sell her house and live in Ireland with her children around her.

Two weeks later she came to Dublin where she stayed with Frances. She was a thin woman with tidy grey hair. She said that her husband had been a brutal, violent man and she described how he had once taken his son's pet mouse and held it over the fire until it burnt to death. She said she had ten children and three miscarriages in thirteen years. One of the children had died. They were so poor that they slept on straw and she had to beg for food. When she found her husband interfering with her eldest daughter she decided to run away because then the authorities would have to take responsibility for the children and they would be better off.

Frances quickly put her right. 'I didn't see why she shouldn't know what it was like for us,' she said later. She told her mother about her childhood in the orphanage: about the beatings, the loneliness, the despair. Her mother cried and said she had no idea it would be like that.

Frances got on with her very well. 'She's soft, like me,' she said, and she invited her to spend Christmas in Dublin. Her mother promised that she would and then returned to England to sell her house and settle her affairs. Frances never saw her again. She wrote to her several times. The letters were returned 'Not known at this address.' She is more bitter and unforgiving about this second rejection than ever she was about the first. She has torn up the cuttings from the newspaper, determined to wipe out all traces of the re-union.

Frances is now married and has three children. She hides, mostly successfully, the scars of her childhood. She keeps going, determined to give her children a better life with less pain and hurt. 'Perhaps I haven't done so badly after all,' she says. 'I'm a survivor, aren't I?'

Part Three

10

A Christian Country

St Joseph's, it was said at the time of the fire, was 'one of the good schools'. Early on we decided that it was outside our field of enquiry to make investigations into other industrial schools or similar institutions such as voluntary orphanages, Catholic or Protestant, because we believed that a thorough study of one place would tell a more effective story. Nevertheless, in the course of our researches we were to receive information, both first and second-hand, about the wider area. Most of what we learned fitted into the same pattern as St Joseph's. Some places seemed to have been worse. A few – so very few – were clearly better.

There was the Booterstown Industrial School in Dublin, whose relaxed atmosphere amazed Sally Johnson on a visit there in the early 1950s, and which the Ryan sisters, sent there when St Joseph's closed, said was quite different and that the children were not beaten. The Morans (who had employed Cissie Meehan) contrasted St Joseph's with St Philomena's orphanage in Dublin which was certified for the reception of boys under seven. In the 1960s, they used to take a child from there on holidays, and, on the first occasion they went to collect him, they arrived unexpectedly. It was, they said, 'charming' with pictures, charts and decorations on all the walls. They saw the dining room, set for the next meal, just four to a table, with tablecloths and mats. The children were having so much fun in the playground that their own youngsters joined in and it was difficult to get them to leave. Their only criticism was the excessive modesty imposed on the children: the little boy would never take off his underpants in the bath.

The criteria we have used in the presentation of the following material is its relevance to the argument that St Joseph's was not unusual either in the manner in which the children were treated, in how their upbringing affected them, or in the abuse of power by an organisation answerable only to itself for its actions.

In early 1976, we wrote a letter to several Irish newspapers asking for information about St Joseph's. One of the replies was from a woman, whom we were unable to meet, but who sent us details of her childhood which she had spent in another industrial school in Dundalk during the 1920s and 1930s, after the death of her parents. It could have been written about Cavan: the floor scrubbing and polishing; the black knitted stockings and boots; the bad food – bread and lard, cocoa made with water, cabbage water soup, apple trees whose fruit was not for the children, an egg once a year on Easter Sunday, no meat and no milk though they 'milked cows and churned butter till we were ready to drop dead' – and the same, all-pervading, fear. 'Everyone in that place scared me stiff. There was no kindness whatsoever, it was so cold, it still haunts me.'

At least she and her friends had some contact with the outside world. They went out to church and for walks (and were laughed at), and she received a good education until she was sixteen. But the cruelty was the same. 'It was a terrible life. The nuns were hard, wicked, unkind. I often wondered were they really God's creatures. I used to pray that my children would not have to suffer like I did and thank God He spared me to them.' She had the equivalent both of a Mother Carmel – 'Mother Gertrude was in charge of us, she was a monster, we were all afraid of her' – and of a Mother Assumpta: 'I always remember Mother Therese. She was nice. She was the exception. The only one. I used just to think of God and of how I would be sixteen one day and then I could get out.' Like so many of those from Cavan, she expressed a Christian charity towards her tormentors: 'I often wonder how they met their God, but I hope he forgave them, as I do.'

It was the fond belief of many of the ex-pupils of St Joseph's that, after their time, things got better. Any who returned after a few years were impressed by the physical improvements, and invariably presumed that this was reflected in the children's treatment. But from accounts we received of girls who had been in institutions in the 1960s and even the early '70s, this would not appear to be the case. We met one woman who had been a godparent to children in an industrial school during this time. At first, she said, she had not been inclined to believe their stories but later, when she found they were consistent, and she did not see how a child could make them up, she believed them. She heard of a child being made to eat its vomit, and of another, denied a drink of water, taking it from the lavatory. These incidents are hearsay and uncorroborated. The reason we give them credence is because we had heard other shocking details about this institution, and knew of identical incidents taking place in St Joseph's.

We knew a woman doctor who had employed a girl in her twenties as a mother's help. Patricia had been brought up in St Vincent's Industrial School in Co. Limerick. At the age of fourteen she was sent to work at a farm where four other girls had been sent before, each one running away for unexplained reasons. Shortly after Patricia started work the farmer made advances to her in the kitchen. She didn't understand what was going on and 'there was this white stuff all over the place' which he told her to clear up. He raped her several times during the following weeks and finally she, too, ran back to the convent – 'Why,' asked our friend 'didn't you tell the nuns?' 'Ma'am, you couldn't tell them that kind of thing. They wouldn't understand.'

For her disobedience in failing to stay at the farm, Patricia was sent to the laundry-reformatory in Limerick. When she left the reformatory she got a job as a domestic but was fired without notice for arguing with the nanny and slept in an old car for a couple of nights. She was picked up by a Canadian who took her to a hotel and she later became pregnant. The baby was adopted. She stayed a year with the doctor before drifting off to London. She has not been heard of since.

We heard Bridget's story from a Mrs Hillery who acted as her godmother during the 1960s when she was at an industrial school run by the Sisters of Charity of Our Lady of Refuge. Mrs Hillery had previously been godmother to a boy from Artane Industrial School, so she was not particularly surprised by the stories of harsh treatment told to her by Bridget and the friends who sometimes came with her. When the girl left school she was put to work as a domestic with a family who did not pay her. Mrs Hillery sent them a bill on Bridget's behalf, and they sent her back to the convent.

She was then found a job in the home of an Irish senator. During the summer he rented his house, together with Bridget's services, to a German family. The wife lost a brooch, claimed that Bridget had stolen it and called the police who took her, then aged seventeen, back to the convent. From there she was sent at once to Limerick where she was met at the station by a police car and taken to the certified reformatory there. Before being taken away she managed to contact Mrs Hillery. She was very distressed and was adamant that she had not stolen the brooch. Mrs Hillery eventually got an admission from the police that Bridget had not stolen the brooch, and that the German woman had decided she had lost it because it had a weak clasp. No charges were laid by the police but the Mother Superior informed Mrs Hillery that Bridget's being sent to the reformatory had nothing to do with the brooch but was because she was 'man-mad'.

Over the next eighteen months, Mrs Hillery did everything she could think of to get Bridget released but all to no avail. Meanwhile she was receiving letters from the girl. It was not only her pitiful pleas for help which were distressing, but their increasing incoherence and disorientation. Mrs Hillery next wrote to Mr Brian Lenihan, then Minister of Education with responsibility for industrial schools. He replied that he had had the case fully investigated and was satisfied that the Reverend Mother had acted in the 'best interests of Bridget's future welfare'.

Finally, Mrs Hillery went to an eminent jurist for assistance. With her, he closely studied all the relevant legislation and then advised her to take a simple course of action. She was to write to Limerick, inform the Mother Superior that she was coming to remove Bridget on a certain date, and then go to collect her. This was done. Bridget was handed over to Mrs. Hillery by a nun who said it was a pity she was going because they intended to make her into a 'Child of Mary' and send her to Galway – presumably to the Magdalen Home for fallen women.

Mrs Hillery was deeply shocked by Bridget's manner and appearance. She was pale, thin and listless, dressed in long, old-fashioned, shabby clothes and seemed to have deteriorated mentally. She said she had worked in the laundry until 7.0 p.m. each day and on Saturday mornings and was paid 25*s*. a week (but no insurance stamps). She said that some of the women had been there for years, and many had been prostitutes. The only meat they had was chicken giblets. Once a week they were taken, under escort, into the town wearing their strange clothes and walking in crocodile. This was 1969.

What makes Bridget's case remarkable is not that a young girl should have been illegally confined but that, alone of all the girls we met, she had someone in the outside world who was willing and able to rescue her.

The story appears to have had a happy ending. After recuperating from her ordeal, Bridget went to England where she took a job as a mother's help with a family who became very fond of her. Although she was semi-literate, they helped her to get training in hotel management. She is now married, has a family and, according to Mrs Hillery, she is happy.

We asked several psychiatrists working in St Brendan's, the largest Dublin mental hospital, about their experience with patients who had been institutionalised. They said, in effect, that the moment they discovered a patient had spent his childhood in an industrial school, there was virtually nothing they could do because the usual emotional development had never taken place. One of the doctors said he had a patient who had been in Artane and had been in and out of the hospital for years. 'He told me he and another boy were once beaten in the washroom for two hours to get a confession of homosexuality out of them following some completely innocent incident. I remember when I was a youngster myself, we'd see these little boys from the industrial school at Cappoquin out walking in line. They didn't behave like kids, there was no life in them, no bounce, their heads hung down. You didn't think about it much at the time because you knew the church was in charge of them.'

Workers at the Simon Community in Dublin told us that at least half of the homeless men who came through their doors had spent their childhood in industrial schools.

In 1976 a priest who runs a hostel in Dublin for boys from such schools compiled figures showing how 108 boys brought up in Artane Industrial School were coping with life. He categorised them in four groups in descending order of vulnerability: normal, borderline (in and out of jobs), social and vocational failures, mentally ill. He found that 22 boys belonged in the first category, 19 boys in the second, 60 in the third and 7 in the fourth.

We have accounts of only two men who spent their childhood in institutions. One of the responses to our letter in the newspapers was from a man who was orphaned as a baby in 1938 and spent his first sixteen years in Nazareth Lodge, a vast, bleak building still standing in Belfast. The boys depended entirely on charity for their support and no regulations, however effectively implemented, protected them. The

Unionist governments which ruled Northern Ireland never interfered with the system by which Roman Catholics provided their own hospitals, schools and orphanages independently of the state.

We went to see Laurence Green in his home in a Catholic ghetto of West Belfast. It was a bleak area: the thickly-wired anti-bomb fencing over an empty block of flats recently occupied by British troops; the anti-British graffitti scrawled obscenely on the wall; the general air of hopelessness and despair. He was tense and strained. His nerves had never been good, he said, and he had a nervous breakdown after his family were thrown out of their previous home at gunpoint by a Protestant terror gang. He had, like many other unskilled Belfast men, been out of work for years. His wife, a calm motherly person, sat with us holding her baby while he told us about the horrors of his childhood.

His earliest memory, he said, was when he was four years old. He had wet and messed himself in bed, and a lay worker shoved his faeces into his mouth while at the same time he was vomiting. He was then put into an ice-cold bath, pushed under with a brush and buckets of cold water poured on to him when he struggled up for air – a usual punishment, he said, for that particular offence which happened a lot because the little children were terrified of getting out of bed in the great, dark dormitory. He remembers being ill quite often: at different times he had jaundice, pleurisy and pneumonia. 'It was the strangest thing, when you were ill it was like Dr Jekyll and Mr Hyde. You got quite different treatment. The nuns came up to see you every day and brought sweets.'

The orphanage was, he said, 'a place of fear – a reign of terror' – terror inflicted by lay workers, nuns and older boys. He showed us a lump on his hand which he had since he was hit with a hurley stick for not getting his answers right in catechism. They were often beaten with hurley sticks, and usually with pants down, even when they got older. 'I've seen terrible things: boys with backsides beaten purple as that sofa. There was a nun that made us undress in front of her and then beat us. That place was so big that you could be screaming at one end and it couldn't be heard at the other. There was one kind nun. She tried to comfort us when we were beaten, but she left when I was ten.' The food consisted of drip-bread and cocoa twice a day, greasy soup with a bit of bad potato for lunch. They got an egg at Easter and a small piece of turkey at Christmas. They wore short-legged dungarees, a shirt and a waistcoat and had no jumpers, even in winter. It was always very cold. 'The place was fumigated with Jeyes fluid – I was beaten once for dropping a bottle of it. We were all very clean, though, baths twice a week.' He said there were bars at the windows and no fire escapes: 'I often thought since how dangerous it was: the place was five storeys high.'

Several times he made the comment that there was 'a lot of homosexuality on the little boys', and finally we asked if he had suffered from this. 'Yes, I did. The first time when I was seven. A gang of older boys raped me. Several of the bigger boys would come on to you.' (After he married, he had been unable to consummate his marriage for over a year.) There was very little supervision of a non-punitive nature. He once saw a boy being forced to slide down the bannisters. He fell off and broke his back. Mr Green admitted that he, too, had 'clobbered' younger boys when he got older.

He attended the school in the orphanage until he was eleven. 'After that I scrubbed, cleaned and did darning and mending.' Some boys were kept on to work on the farm, which belonged to Nazareth Lodge, until they were twenty-one. 'I'd write a book about the place myself, but I haven't the education.'

During the years he and his older brother were there, none of their surviving grandparents, or any other relations, ever came to see them or wrote to them. He had heard that his brother, who was no longer a Catholic, now belonged to a Protestant extremist organisation. He said he had once come across a man who had been brought up in the local Dr Barnardo's Home, and they had compared their experiences. 'They had some homosexuality there, but nothing like at Nazareth, and it was quite different: they had good food, and clothes and so on. They lacked for nothing because the Orange Lodges looked after them.' He reckoned that around 1952 conditions improved a little – they began to get sausages occasionally. 'I think the government must have begun to interfere.'

Peter Tyrrell was almost the same age as Laurence Green. He had spent a number of years in an industrial school run by the Christian brothers in Letterfrack, Co. Galway. He was known to several of our acquaintances because of his part in the preparation of a report on industrial schools in the 1960s. He was at Letterfrack during the 1930s, and had tried to write a book about his childhood there,[1] but was unable to express himself coherently. He claimed that the boys were sometimes stripped and beaten while naked for long periods and that he was sodomised by one of the Brothers. When he told a priest in confession about this, the reply was: 'How dare you speak so of the Brothers. If it wasn't for them you wouldn't have a roof over your head.' Peter Tyrrell volunteered for the war in 1939 and was taken prisoner. He told one of our informants that prison camp was a tea-party compared with his childhood. Letterfrack, he said, was 'like Belsen' – the same comment that was made to us by Hannah about St Joseph's in the 1930s.

Laurence Green walked back with us over the torn-up paving stones to the place where a bus route once passed, but where the only public transport is now provided by shabby group taxis plying in and out from the city centre. He pointed out the scars of the last ten years like a wall with gaping holes gouged by the bullets which had torn the life out of a Provo some weeks before.

'Of course,' he said, 'Nazareth isn't like that any more. You wouldn't recognise it now inside, and the nuns are altogether different. They've set it up as a home for children whose families have suffered from the Troubles. It's all different now, but what worries me is what would happen if Ireland was re-united. It would happen all over again and no-one would dare to interfere.'

In 1980 the *Irish Independent* published a story about alleged sexual offences which had taken place in the Protestant-run Kincora Boys Home in East Belfast. It was later discovered that one of the house-fathers in the home was a practising homosexual and the *Irish Times* later revealed that RUC detectives had been prevented from investigating offences against Kincora boys as long ago as 1974. A file prepared by detectives then, and sent to RUC headquarters, was later found to have been lost. A subsequent RUC investigation led to the jailing of the home's three housefathers in December 1981. The three men pleaded guilty to twenty-eight charges of sexual offences against boys in their care at Kincora.

In his judgment at the trial, the Lord Chief Justice, Lord Lowry, expressed surprise that such offences were allowed to go on at a publicly-run children's home for nearly twenty years.

For those who wish to believe that all has now changed for the better, that children in care are no longer ill-treated and that children's homes are subject to adequate inspection, the following facts which emerged at the Kincora Tribunal of Inquiry in 1984 will be of interest. It was revealed, for example, that the inspection duties of the Social Work Advisory Group had been carried out irregularly, with some homes not having been visited for five years. This was despite a recommendation in 1976 that homes should be visited annually. Spot checks were unusual and the usual procedure was for homes to be given three weeks' notice of an impending inspection. In the case of Kincora no inspection reports were available for 1969, 1970 and 1971.

Reference was also made to Williamstown House Children's Home in North Belfast where the principal, an Anglican lay monk, had been convicted of sex offences against the boys in 1981. In 1978 an inspector reported an atmosphere of 'freedom, friendliness and happiness' there. Williamstown House has since been closed.

11

Investigation

All children need love, care and security if they are to develop into full and mature persons.

Kennedy Report 1970

Since Ireland gained its independence, three reports have been published on the subject of the country's industrial and reformatory schools: the Cussen Report in 1936, the Tuarim Report in 1966 and the Kennedy Report in 1970.

Of the three, the Kennedy Report was by far the most important in that it made recommendations which would bring the residential care of children in Ireland into line with modern thinking. But the other two reports are also worth considering in some detail. They represented a brave attempt to improve the system which was responsible for the care of thousands of Irish children but, at the same time, they seemed to avoid accepting unpalatable truths. From even a cursory inspection of a few institutions, it must have been apparent to the worthy men and women who sat on the committees which compiled these reports that the very children whose lot they were seeking to improve were suffering restrictions in their mental and physical development which would reap a terrible harvest in their adult life. The committees relied for much of their information on reports from authoritative figures, regarding with a certain degree of suspicion first-hand accounts from those who had been through the system. At all times they avoided overt criticism of those responsible for the children, pointing out that the church was undertaking an onerous task with very little reward.

The Cussen Report resulted from a commission set up to inquire into and report on the schools. Their brief included the care and education of the children, after-care and staffing. At that time there were fifty-two industrial schools in the country, certificated for the reception of 6,563 children. All were under Roman Catholic management.[2] The commission had nine members: Geoffrey Cussen (Chairman), Chairman of the Dublin District Court; Mrs Mary Hackett, who was later to serve on the Tribunal of Inquiry into the Cavan fire; Senator Mrs Clarke, widow of the Rebellion figure executed in 1916; a parish priest and two civil servants (one of whom was the Deputy Chief Inspector of the Department of Education), a doctor and two laymen.

They heard evidence from invited representatives from the relevant departments of state – Education, Justice and Local Government – and from interested organisations, including the Catholic Rescue and Protection Society, the National Society for the Prevention of Cruelty to Children, the Provincial of the Irish Christian Brothers who ran most of the seniors boys' industrial schools, and representatives of the trade unions. Among others who gave submissions were Madame Maude Gonne McBride, the famous Anglo-Irish revolutionary, Miss Margaret McNeill (whose visits were recalled by girls of St Joseph's at that time), and managers and teachers from seven industrial schools, nine of which the commission visited.

They found that the children were suitably housed, fed and clothed and that their treatment was, in general, kindly and humane although they made detailed suggestions for improved medical care. They wanted the children to receive 'at least' as good an education as children outside, criticised the tendency to give formal instruction in the evenings and wished each manager to make every pupil feel that 'he is his guardian and friend while maintaining an ever-vigilant but unobtrusive discipline.'

They pointed out that it was in the interests of the managers to keep up the numbers of children in their schools. This was because running expenses did not diminish in direct proportion to the numbers of children in the institutions.[3] They disliked the practice, in some schools, of having silence at meals and in workrooms and they deplored the lack of recreation facilities: '. . . monotonous marching round a school yard takes the place of free play.' In contrast, one school was singled out for praise. 'We have learned with pleasure that the Conductors of one Industrial School, Drogheda Junior Boys, in charge of the French Sisters of Charity, have provided a camp of wooden huts at Termonfeckin, to which they have taken all their charges for a month's holiday at the seaside during each of the past two years. The Sisters expressed the opinion that the resulting benefits in the health and spirits of the children and the widening of their experience more than repaid the trouble and expense entailed.' The destiny of many of these little boys on reaching the age of ten would have been Artane.

They did not comment on the rule by which children could be sent from industrial to reformatory schools, nor about the punishments received by the children, although, being covered by the regulations, this would have been within their field of reference. Nor did they make any reference to the rise in the mortality rate.[4]

On the whole they approved the continuation of the system. 'Subject to various changes, the present system affords the most suitable method of dealing with these children. . . . We specially recommend that the management of schools by Religious Orders who have undertaken that work should continue.'

In 1966, thirty years on from the Cussen Report and a year before the last girls left St Joseph's, a pamphlet was published by members of a branch of Tuarim, an independent association which, during the 1960s, produced a series of authoritative and influential studies on Irish affairs with the stated object of informing public opinion. The pamphlet was called *Some of Our Children – A Report on the Residential Care of the Deprived Child in Ireland*. Its intention was to pressure for reform in this area.

There were nine members of the group, all lay people. One of them was Peter Tyrrell, described as 'ex-pupil industrial school'. He was not, however, one of the three compilers of the final report.

An important change which had taken place was that a number of children were now admitted – as opposed to being committed – to residential care through the Department of Health Acts, by which means they could be sent to voluntary homes as well as to industrial schools, and more easily fostered out.[5] Tuarim noted, however, that in spite of the passing of adoption laws in 1952, many children were still being left in institutional care from babyhood; a situation which, they said, would be unacceptable in the United Kingdom. They commented on the fact that in England and Wales 45 per cent as opposed to 29 per cent of children in care were boarded out and observed that child care sevices in Ireland were 'noticeable by their absence.'

What they described as the most valuable part of their work were the visits they made to nine industrial schools and two reformatories. They also met ex-industrial school pupils and the responsible authorities. Out of this they made a number of comments and recommendations.

They noted that the committal of the children from one family to different schools, particularly if one parent was dead 'often means the virtual disintegration of the family as a unit'. Concern was expressed about the lack of interest by the staff at some of the schools in maintaining children's links – 'which can be gradually weakened and break' – with whatever relatives they had in the outside world. The attitude was, 'The child is well looked after here. What does he want to worry about his parents for?'

They found a profusion of toys for small children in the schools, though only one school had any sign of books. They noted approvingly that 'All the convent schools we visited were meticulously clean and tidy.' They were impressed with the physical appearance of the girls but made the point that just because they appeared 'docile and manageable, this was not necessarily good for them. . . provided the children are physically healthy, well-clothed, obedient and can speak Irish, officialdom is satisfied.'

Attention was drawn to the lack of legislation covering voluntary homes. 'In theory anyone can kidnap a child, walk up to a home or a certified school which accepts voluntary admissions, tell a plausible story and get the child taken in. We find this disquieting.'[6]

They described the difficulties experienced by boys and girls when they left the schools and the lack of after-care. They said that a lack of sex education resulted in the children being in a state of total ignorance; there was a lack of knowledge of ordinary family life and social behaviour, with no one to turn to for advice. Girls, they felt, were especially vulnerable. Brief case histories were given of two girls, both of whom had illegitimate babies, one of whom had been claimed without difficulty by her mother at fourteen, taken to England and then been abandoned.[7]

Some of their comments were oddly at variance with what we had learned from the girls at St Joseph's: 'Many of the girls go on to secondary or vocational schools, take their intermediate and leaving certificates or attend secretarial courses. If they have ability they seem to have a reasonable choice of career open to them: nursing, secretarial work, civil service, air hostess. Because of their early environment and heredity, not all the girls are capable of benefitting from these opportunities. . . . Some will be mentally backward or educationally retarded. Residential domestic work is the only employment in Ireland for such girls.'

They expressed confidence in the managers of the schools. 'In the circumstances, financial and physical, the managers perform a task which no-one else would contemplate. They do all and more than can be reasonably expected with too little help or support. . . . When a child leaves an industrial school to take up employment, he is equipped with a suitcase and at least two complete sets of clothes as well as toilet requisites. . . . everything is supplied by the school at its expense.'

We think of those like Frances, who when she left St Joseph's a year after the publication of this pamphlet was, to her humiliation, not wearing a bra, had no coat and carried her few bits of clothing in a paper bag.

The Tuarim Report included a paragraph about St Joseph's, Limerick, run by the Sisters of the Good Shepherd, where Bridget was illegally detained in 1968. 'This school was not visited by members of the group but we have heard excellent reports of it. . . . The girls receive education and training which enables them to take up responsible positions, notably in nursing and commerce, when they leave.'[8] A somewhat different career structure than that envisaged for Bridget, whose destination was to be the Magdalen laundry in Galway.

The report continued: 'The mentally retarded and socially maladjusted who will be unable to organise their lives without the support of an institution or a protective family. . . are found unskilled work in the institution run by the same religious order. . . some of them work in laundries run by the convent. . . .' What is meant by 'socially maladjusted' is unclear.

In this area, the report accepted a state of affairs in which girls could be deprived of liberty for years, or possibly life, for the 'crime' of giving birth to a baby out of wedlock or of being mentally backward.

Commenting on punishment they found that, as far as girls were concerned, 'experienced female staff have little difficulty in coping with young girls without resorting to punitive measures at all.' On the boys' institutions: 'We have received accounts from a number of former pupils alleging excessive corporal punishment in the past. We have also heard stories of recent punishments which we consider to be either unsuitable or excessive. In the absence of any verification that the alleged punishments took place in the form described, they must be treated as hypothetical.'

Their recommendations were excellent and represented progressive thinking on child care. They wanted the 1908 Act replaced; the Department of Health to take over responsibility for all children in care from the Departments of Education and Justice; they wanted institutional care to be abolished and replaced with children's homes, in keeping with contemporary ideas of small, mixed-sex units, and a proper aftercare service to be set up.

But it had all come too late for Peter Tyrrell and too much of the reality had been ignored. Perhaps his involvement in the Tuarim study was for him a final hope, the channel through which his protest at the horror of his childhood and that of other children would be heard at last. He would not believe the members of the group when they assured him that things were better now. He can have had little feeling that the truth had been told, the record put straight and justice done. A year after the publication of the Tuarim pamphlet he committed suicide by setting himself alight on London's Hampstead Heath.[9]

In 1967, the year that St Joseph's Orphanage was closed, the Fianna Fail government set up a committee to carry out a survey of reformatory and industrial schools. The chairman was District Justice Eileen Kennedy, and there were eleven other members; the Christian Brother Manager of Artane School, a psychiatrist, a nun with qualifications in social science, four representatives of departments of state, three laymen and a laywoman.

The committee covered an enormous amount of ground. They met formally on sixty-nine occasions; they commissioned surveys and they visited all the schools at least once, as well as local authority children's homes and foster homes. The result was a comprehensive, compassionate and authoritative report, embodying modern attitudes towards the overall needs of children, both emotional and physical, with recommendations which repeated and extended those of the Tuarim Report.[10] It laid stress on the provision for children in residential care of educational facilities superior to those obtaining generally, and on the importance of providing after-care facilities. 'Heretofore, much of the emphasis has been on the provision of creature comforts and accommodation for children, and on safeguarding them from moral and physical dangers. Too little emphasis has been placed on the child's needs to enable him to develop into maturity and to adjust himself satisfactorily to the society in which he lives.'

One of their recommendations was for an end to the capitation grant in favour of a block grant. The former arrangement, they said, resulted in schools being unwilling to permit children to leave or be transferred. One manager actually told the committee that he could not 'afford to release children' for that reason.[11] This problem had been identified thirty-four years before by Cussen. They remarked on the children's lack of contact with the outside world. 'We met children who did not know that food had to be paid for or that letters had to be stamped.'

The report was refreshingly honest and showed a real desire to effect change. Yet, at the same time, the committee was anxious to avoid apportioning blame. 'In listing the limitations of the present child care system insofar as it concerns Reformatory and Industrial Schools, it may seem that we are criticising those responsible for the schools.[12] This is not the intention of this committee: indeed we are very much aware that if it were not for the dedicated work of many of our religious bodies, the position would be a great deal worse than it is now.'

The committee attempted to contact all known voluntary residential homes outside the state system (including those like the Poor Clares' baby home at Stamullen), but did not receive replies from all of them. Thus they were unable to supply accurate figures and other information about them. They recommended inspection of these homes and said that without this 'such a home could stagnate', adding, 'we are not suggesting that many of these homes are not well run.'

They criticised the inspection of industrial schools as being 'so far as we can judge, totally ineffective. . . . We are satisfied that the State obligation to inspect these schools at least once a year has not always been fulfilled.'

At no point did the Kennedy Report express concern over the suitability of celibates as mother and father figures; although it did say that 'The ideal situation would be that the housemother should look after the running of the unit and the housefather should go out to work in the usual way.' Possibly this did imply that religious were not considered suitable for this role, but this was as far as the committee went.

In the area of reformatories the Kennedy Report was courageously prepared to expose the long-hidden scandal of illegal detention in the laundry-reformatories, certified and otherwise, and Magdalen Homes. They found an average of twenty-six girls being held in the two girls' certified reformatories – one of which was St Joseph's, Limerick – during the period 1964-9. They said that about 15 per cent of those 'detained' were 'voluntary' cases who had been admitted at the request of relatives, clergy or Health Authorities. Certain types of offenders (girls known to have been prostitutes, or who on conviction were found to be pregnant were not, they said, accepted by these institutions. Of the non-certified institutions, they said 'a number of girls considered by parents, relatives, social workers, welfare officers, clergy or gardaí to be in moral danger or uncontrollable are also accepted in these convents for a period on a *voluntary* basis. . . . [our italics]. This method of voluntary arrangement. . . can be criticised on a number of grounds. It is a haphazard system, its legal validity is doubtful, and the girls admitted in this irregular way, and not being aware of their rights, may remain for long periods and become, in the process, unfit for re-emergence into society.

'In the past, many girls have been taken into these convents and confined there all their lives. . . . No State grants are payable for the maintenance of those in voluntary Magdalen institutions. . . there is consequently no State control or right of inspection of these institutions.'

From this it can surely be deduced that everything we heard about 'poor Katy O'Toole', sent from St Joseph's to the Magdalen Home in Galway and kept there for a quarter of a century, as well as about Bridget, detained in the Reformatory in Limerick, was only too true.[13]

The committee commissioned a survey from Rev. Father O'Doherty, Professor of Logic and Psychology at University College, Dublin, whose Department of Psychology conducted it. Using standard tests for the measurement of intelligence, perceptual ability, verbal reasoning, literacy and numeracy they found far higher levels of mental handicap, educational retardation and backwardness among industrial school children than among the Irish population at large. They also found that, whereas a high incidence of mental handicap was not marked among younger girls, by the time they had reached the age of fifteen it was 38.8 per cent higher. 'It is difficult,' the writers of the survey comment, 'to say why this should be so.'

Discussing the terms of reference for this survey, the committee stated: 'Research on the topic shows that the most important factor in childhood and later development is the quality and quantity of personal relationships available to the child. . . . If it is seen from a study of our institutions of care that our children have not a competence in these areas of development which is up to the standard attained by the majority of the population, then we can speak of cultural deprivation in such institutions as a fact. . . . Such a statement would have no implications as to the conditions which obtain within our institutions.'

Who can be surprised that Peter Tyrrell despaired?

12

An Abdication of Responsibility

In St Joseph's Orphanage in Cavan, throughout the period about which there is first-hand evidence, it would appear that both the Children's Act and the Industrial School Regulations were broken, and that the system designed to prevent abrogation of the rules consistently failed to work. The Department of Education's Industrial Schools section did not enforce its own regulations and – as was admitted by the Kennedy Report – there were deficiencies in the attitude of their Inspectors who annually produced those unperturbed, congratulatory reports.

In practical terms, the irregularities covered every aspect of the mental and physical development of the children. They failed to receive the nourishing food laid down for them in the dietary scale. Their clothing was inadequate, certainly until the mid-60s. Punishment far exceeded the rules and was not reported to the authorities as specified. They were sent out to work when they should have been at school. Some of them were confined for the whole of their adult life in laundry-reformatories of dubious legality. On the other hand, the legislation, in many instances, actually permitted and endorsed a restrictive and punitive approach towards the girls. It was the law which, in the 1930s, made it possible to put Mary MacHenry who 'liked to put a quiff into her hair' and who pulled off a nun's veil, into the reformatory in Limerick. Similarly with Lal Smith in the 1950s – the girl described as having 'no harm in her' and who 'used to make the others laugh'. If Martha Prendergast had run away when she was sent to live with the farming couple in 1960 at the age of thirteen and the man made sexual advances to her, she could, according to the provisions of a 1957 addition to the main Act, have been sent to a reformatory. (This actually happened to a girl from another industrial school under similar circumstances – see Chapter 10.)

When Martha was sent back to the convent, she was beaten by the nuns. This beating – and all the others – should, according to the regulations, have been put down in the School Journal, and notified to the Department. There is no evidence that this was done or that when Mary McNeill and Joan Thomas were sent out to work that this was done through the formalities required by the Act in the event of a child being sent out on licence to live with 'a trustworthy and respectable person' or for a course of training.

It would appear that the Acts and regulations which were there to protect the children were broken, yet when they were punitive and restrictive they were fully implemented. This situation had existed for decades in a democracy with an independent judiciary and a professional, permanent civil service. The responsibility for such children lay with both church and state. Each had abdicated that responsibility.

The attitude of the Poor Clare nuns to our investigations, perhaps understandably, was one of reluctance and evasion. In March 1975 we wrote to the convent in Cavan to ask if we could see the orphanage and talk to some of the Sisters. When our letter was not answered we telephoned and were given permission to visit.

We were shown into the convent parlour where we were joined by Sister Benedict and Sister Assumpta. Sister Benedict did most of the talking. At first she concentrated on the fire, clearly a focal point in her memory. 'The Department used to send inspectors. They'd come without notice. Before the fire there was a Miss McNeill. In 1960 the Department sent out an instruction that orphanages were to be phased out so less children were sent. Sister Assumpta gave them a great training in laundry, and they also got training in housework and needlework. A nun would do the cooking, helped by the older children. The orphans usually went out to domestic work and we placed them in jobs at sixteen. Fifteen or sixteen of them went to the nuns. Eight went to England to the Loretto Order. The girls were mostly illegitimate and they were the happiest little creatures you could wish to meet.

'They were well-mannered and well-educated. I suppose we were like a strict boarding school. Sometimes they would try to run out. I never met the like of their loyalty to the nuns – they could not speak better of us behind our backs.' We asked why the children should not have spoken well of them. 'Well, they could have spoken about the strictness.' We asked if the girls were ever chastised. 'Only by the principals,' Sister Benedict replied. 'There was a lovely family spirit, just lovely, although we did have to have the strictness. We spoke of them as "our children". They weren't difficult. Just ordinary disobedience. They were not simple, not one was mentally retarded. They come back to visit us with their little babies and seem very happily married.'

Sister Assumpta, who figured in so many girls' memories for her kindness and who gave Sally a mother's love, spoke mainly about her work in the laundry. 'A set of them worked with me and I carried coal and broke sticks with them. They were great children. So gifted. I really loved them. Thank God I never lifted a hand to them.'

A couple of months later, one sunny afternoon, we drove out to the Poor Clares home for babies at Stamullen, not far from Dublin, where, Sister Benedict had told us, Sister Anne (who, with Sister Catherine, had been in charge of the girls from the mid-50s to the mid-60s) was now working. The home was a solid Victorian country house set in large and immaculately kept grounds. A girl opened the locked door and went to get the Matron while we waited in the very clean and polished parlour. It was very quiet.

We explained to the Matron that we were writing a book about the Cavan orphanage and would like to meet Sister Anne. The Matron, a brisk woman with keys on a chain round her waist, said that she was now in another Poor Clare convent. We asked the Matron if she knew any of the girls who had been in Cavan, mentioning one whom we had heard was working in Stamullen. That girl had left, she replied, and it would be better not to disturb her. She did not like people to know where she had come from. Indeed, when a couple of St Joseph's girls had come to visit her, she had become 'almost hysterical' and said she wanted nothing more to do with the orphanage. Our conversation with the Matron was brief. Later we were told that she was Sister Theresa, one of the last two nuns in charge of the children in Cavan.

Soon afterwards we visited the convent where the Matron had said we would find Sister Anne. She said she would have to go and ask her Superior's permission for the interview. Before doing this she asked whether we had chosen to write about Cavan because of the fire. 'The Sisters were blamed, you know, because none of them died, only the children. There was a lot of controversy about it. That place should never have been re-built. Things went on there which should not have happened. I tried to change things, make them better, but there was a lot of opposition to what I tried to do.'

She left the room to speak to her Mother Superior. When she returned she said she had been instructed that interviews were not permitted. Any questions we had should be written down and sent to the Order's Counsellor. We prepared a list of basic questions about food, finance for the girls and clothing and sent them to the Counsellor. We received no reply. We then sent the list to Sister Anne who said she could not answer them fully because it was many years since she had been in Cavan.

A year later we tried to see the orphanage records. We telephoned the convent in Cavan and were told that the house was in mourning for Sister Carmel who had just died. We must write to the Mother General, they said, for permission. Some weeks later the Mother General telephoned in answer to our letter. She said she had heard about the book, and wanted to give us her support. The orphanage had been closed before she became Mother General; she disliked the system of institutional orphanages and would never have countenanced them. Although she was an American herself, she had met girls who had been brought up in industrial schools and she knew how they damaged people. We must understand that the nuns who ran them had not been trained in child care.

We pointed out that the Department of Education were not without blame and had given very little money to finance the care of the children. She said that if the system was bad, then this must mean that the people who ran it were also at fault. 'If you are going to indict the system,' she said, 'you must indict my nuns as well.'

She said that we could not have access to the orphanage records because of the question of confidentiality but she wished us success with our project and said it might be possible to meet with us later in the year. 'We must accept whatever you write with humility,' she said, 'and regard it as a burden which has been sent to try us.'

We wrote to her again asking if it would be possible to see the Rules and Regulations under which St Joseph's had been certificated, and a few examples of the orphanage accounts. She telephoned to say that it would not be possible to see the accounts because they were not kept 'in those days'. She suggested that we meet Sisters Theresa, Cecilia and Anne, a parish priest and the Bishop in Cavan, and two older Sisters in the convent. 'It is a pity that you could not meet Sister Carmel. She died a short time ago. She was such a cultured person, so interested in literature and drama. She'd tell you how marvellous our freedom is today – to go to the theatre and so on.'

We attempted to do as she suggested. The Bishop of Kilmore, with cordiality, pointed out that the orphanage had closed some time before he attained his present position, and he knew nothing about it. We arranged to meet the priest in Dublin, but he cancelled our appointment and did not make another. We tried to meet with the Sisters but were asked first to contact the Mother General.

She telephoned us in a quite different tone. 'I don't think I can permit you to talk to my Sisters now. I had not earlier seen your letter to the newspapers and it is clear from it that you are prejudiced against the Order and that nothing constructive could come from any meetings. You do not have an open mind on the subject. . . your motives are cash and sensationalism.' It was thus impossible to give the Sisters who had looked after the children an opportunity to state their point of view.

A number of girls from St Joseph's were sent to the laundry run by the Sisters of Our Lady of Charity of Refuge in Gloucester Street. We had never been able to contact any of them and all we knew of it were Ann-Marie's still horrified memories of what she had seen as a twelve-year-old in 1960: the crop-haired women, wearing sacking, sweating in the steam.

We had never been able to discover under what section of the 1908 Act girls were transfered to Gloucester Street, or if they had gone under licence. We telephoned the convent and made an appointment to see Sister Angela. Gloucester Street is in the inner-city area and the convent is a typical Victorian institution. Sister Angela, a trained social worker, was an authoritative figure, intelligent and competent. We quote extensively from her interview.

'This type of institution was set up during the last century in response to inadequacies in the social services to provide a type of custodial care for delinquent women and girls.[15] There were people who needed protection. People who – as they used to say moralistically – "fell from the paths of righteous virtue" – and were not suitable for mental hospitals or county homes. An unmarried mother, particularly in the Irish countryside, was a pariah. She couldn't stay indefinitely in a Mother and Baby Home, and she couldn't return to her family. She would either become an unmarried mother again and again, or would literally die in the streets because she had no-one to take care of her.

'Some of them came from very good families. There are women in this House who were from a better social class than I was. Some of them went with a man just once and became pregnant. You cannot be too hard on the families, you have to think of the social climate of the time. But they are not all unmarried mothers. There is still a need for a refuge and some of the backlog is still here.'

'Did they come voluntarily or were they sent?'

'Well, that's debatable. What is voluntary and what is being sent? There was no legal provision by which they were sent and there was no legal provision by which they stayed.'

'It was never custodial?'

'No, completely voluntary, in the sense that they did not have to come or have to remain. . . earlier the criteria for the treatment of girls was preservative and protecting, preventing them from becoming delinquent. It was never punitive, though in those times there may have been punitive aspects.

'We began to separate them into groups in 1964. We always did have young girls but they lived in the ordinary institution with the others until it became appropriate. We usually have a section with the old-age pensioners – ex-alcoholics, street walkers, and some who were unable to cope. Then we have a group with those who were mentally retarded unmarried mothers, and another group with those who are middle-aged who were delinquents, women with problems. We also have the women from industrial schools who were inadequate. The schools knew they weren't going to be able to cope and that unless they were looked after they would become delinquents and alcoholics. This was where the preventitive aspect came in.'[16]

She said they now had a training centre for ten girls, of whom five were usually on remand from the courts, and the others were from the Departments of Education and Health. 'When they come from Education, it means from what were the industrial schools. Usually they are sent here because they are very difficult: they are acting out and may be bullies. They settle down better among their own age group. We have never taken anyone under thireen – earlier it used to be the late teens and twenties. Recently it is down to thirteen and fourteen. The programme now for the younger girls is half-training, half-education. Education is in the morning now. It used to be at night. They do a couple of hours in the laundry three afternoons a week. When the girls leave they often go through a wild stage but will come back at a later date – we often have to keep them till they are twenty-two or twenty-three. You don't like to be over-protective, but you can't throw them out into the world until they can cope.'[17]

We asked her about several of the Cavan girls whom we were told had been sent to Gloucester Street in the late 50s and early 60s. This, she said, would have been before her time. But she did remember one – Therese Dwyer. 'She tried to burn down the place. She was very disturbed. We used to get a lot of girls from industrial schools, but this has changed. A lot of the Homes are looking after their past pupils better, they have better chances of education and are not just thrown into the world at sixteen.'

She thought the turning point for children in care had been the publication of the Kennedy Report: 'Though to be quite honest I think it was obsolete before it was published. It came at a time when there was an upsurge into child care anyway. It slated some of the industrial schools wholesale, but the changes were already taking place.[18] We all know there were terrible things, but it annoys me slightly when society gets up on its high-horse and says, "Oh, the way the nuns were looking after the girls!", but they didn't want us to look after them in any other way. The type of care you get in any society reflects the society in which you live.'

We asked Sister Angela under what section of the Act industrial school girls would have been sent to the convent, prior to its present official certification by the Department of Education. She said she could not remember exactly what section, but that it was a clause which permitted children to be sent away for special courses and special education. We asked how this was financed. Their grants, she replied, were transferred by the schools.

Although a 1957 amendment to the 1908 Act does state that, during a period of detention, an industrial school manager may grant a leave of absence to attend a course of instruction at another school either as a boarder or a day pupil, it is difficult to see how these requirements were fulfilled at Gloucester Street or similar institutions. The 'course of training' could hardly have applied to the laundry since they were already trained in the laundry at Cavan. In effect, although it was never specified, Gloucester Street and similar uncertified institutions operated as reformatories.

As for those other women, now no longer young – some of whom were still in Gloucester Street – who had been sent there for 'preventitive and preservative' reasons, we could find no legal process by which they were put into this 'custodial-type' care, when the period of their committal orders ended at the age of sixteen. Many of them, as a result, were institutionalised for life.

Much later we met a woman who had worked for the Co. Cavan Health Authority during the early 1960s, administering the 1953 Health Act.[19] She said that only under rare circumstances, and for short-term stays, were 'Health Act' children put into St Joseph's. It was considered, she said, a 'last resort'. She had visited the orphanage mainly on the few occasions when children admitted by her department were there. She had, however, gone to complain several times when her office had not been notified that girls had left. Even though they were committed through the Department of Education, their after-care was the responsibility of her department. On one occasion when this happened she recalled a Mother Abbess sweeping out of the room saying, 'Just you try prosecuting me!' She said that this Mother Abbess would not let her go straight into the orphanage. 'She didn't like it. They'd give you tea in the parlour all right, but they didn't want you to go any further. You have to remember that the church was a law unto itself.'

We told this woman that, according to evidence we had received from the girls, some of them had been sent out to work before their committal periods were up. She was astonished to hear this. She said that the grants for all the girls, whether under the Department of Health or Education, passed through the local office where she had worked. She was absolutely sure that, according to the returns, none of them had officially left St Joseph's before the age of release at sixteen.

Our first contact with the Department of Education, Special Schools Section, took place in 1975. We were given every possible assistance in finding the documentation we were seeking. A young clerk made a list of the legislation which the department administered. We photostated the 1908 Children's Act and the report of the inquiry into the Cavan fire, both of which were unobtainable outside the department.'[20]

A year later we had a meeting with the civil servant in charge of the

Special Schools Section with responsibility for what were industrial schools but which, since 1970, have been re-named 'Residential Homes'. We had written to three of these Homes asking whether we could visit them. The managers had referred our request to the civil servant in question. He said the Homes were private. We pointed out that they were certificated and in receipt of public money. 'We all try to do our best for the children,' he said, adding that he could see no point in writing about a fire which had taken place thirty years before. 'Surely you should write about what would help the children now, and how can your book do that?'

He said that he had not been in charge during any of the period covered by our book and that he and his colleagues were working 'round the clock' attempting to implement all the (1970) Kennedy Report recommendations. We asked who had been in charge. He said none were around: one person was in England and others were dead.

To our more detailed questions he said the answers were not available. We asked about children being sent out to work. He said it was not possible to see 'individual confidential reports'. He 'believed' that accounts were not audited. At the mention of Gloucester Street he said, 'I don't think we'd better delve into that terrain,' and, as though excusing his department, said it was not certificated.

Much later we had a discussion with an administrative officer in the department, who had recently been given responsibility for Residential Homes. He told us that the civil servant whom we had met had been transferred. 'He was an industrial schools inspector for years, you know.'

Over a period of some months we tried to contact Dr Anna McCabe, the now retired Medical Inspector for Girls Industrial Schools and Reformatories, but were always informed that she was away. We tried to meet the retired National Schools Inspector for the Cavan area. He refused to see us, saying that 'the nuns did their best for the children'. Formal interviews were requested with those (still living) who had exercised ultimate government control: the Ministers for Education. All refused. The names of the Ministers up to 1968 are: Eoin McNeill (one term); J. M. O'Sullivan (four terms); Richard Mulcahy (two terms); Sean Moylan (one term); Thomas Derrig (seven terms); Sean T. O'Ceallaigh (one term); Eamonn de Valera (one term); Jack Lynch (one term); Patrick J. Hillery (two terms); George Colley (one term); Donogh

O'Malley (two terms); Brian Lenihan (one term). Three of them became Presidents of the Republic: Eamonn de Valera, Sean T. O'Ceallaigh and Patrick J. Hillery, who is the present incumbent. Jack Lynch was Prime Minister from 1966-73 and 1977-9.

We were, however, granted an interview with Padraig Faulkner, Minister for Education in the Fianna Fáil government from 1969-73. This covered the period of the Kennedy Report in 1970, although it was not until 1973, under the Coalition government, that it was the subject of debate in either houses of Dáil Éireann, and then it was in the Senate – a reflection of the urgency and importance accorded the issue. It was also during Mr Faulkner's period in office that the process of replacing orphanages with group homes continued. This change, however, was not initiated by the state authority, but by the late Bishop of Kilkenny, the Rev. Dr Birch, who took a leading role in social reform in Ireland.

Mr Faulkner claimed that the first thing he had done as Minister was to visit a boys' reformatory. 'The staff were doing a good job in spite of the old buildings and bad facilities.' He had ordered a new Special School[21] to be built to replace it. We reminded him that we had come to see him about industrial schools, not reformatories. 'Same thing,' he said. 'I saw them all as deprived children.' But it was not the same thing. Former pupils of industrial schools had always suffered from the association in the public mind with those who had broken the law and who had gone to reformatories.[22] Mr Faulkner could not agree.

'I started with the premise that the child was not bad. I set up Residential Homes instead of orphanages, and brought in the idea of having men as well as women in charge. I cannot take the credit for what I did, and I cannot answer for what my predecessors did or said, but, on the other hand, I support them. Times change, the electorate and attitudes of society alter. What was possible by the time I was in power would not have been possible before. I probably would not have tried to make the changes that I did had I been in power at an earlier time.'

We spoke about the laws and regulations which seemed to have been broken. 'You've got to remember that attitudes have changed,' he said. 'Before Vatican II it was a matter of the individual and his faith. Now we have learned to be more concerned with the total community: with all human beings.' He enlarged on the subject of changes in the spiritual life. 'Some things were taboo then which are acceptable now. . . my predecessor brought in free secondary education in 1967 – you have to bear that in mind when you talk about these children not getting a good education.'

We mentioned the lack of nourishing food. 'If you remember, teenagers are always hungry,' he replied. 'I was brought up on a farm and things were not easy for anyone. People forget this, and you can't judge yesterday by today's physical standards.' We pointed out that our 'yesterday' had only ended in 1967 in Cavan. 'You must,' he said, 'be objective.'

He denied any knowledge of girls being sent to non-certificated reformatories. On being told that they had often been sent away to work from an early age he said, 'I'm not accepting that happened. I could not believe that.' He wondered if we had ever talked to anyone who had something good to say about industrial schools. 'I only got one complaint about a Residential Home,' he said. 'I investigated it at once in person. I asked around and it was completely without foundation.' What was the nature of the complaint? 'It was about cleanliness,' said Mr Faulkner.

Epilogue

We asked Clare to keep in touch with us, but did not hear from her for almost two years. Then she telephoned to say that she and the child were going to England, to a live-in housekeeping job, and she would like to see us before she went. She also mentioned that she wanted to go back to St Joseph's one last time, so we offered to drive her. She looked tired and strained. She had found it hard to find work and was constantly in debt. She was going to England as a last resort.

We arrived in Cavan on a cold, bleak day in March. The yard doors of the convent were open and well-dressed young mothers were chatting to a nun and bringing small children out from the national school. The two nuns who came into the parlour to talk to us were teachers. They did not recognise Clare and laughed in disbelief as, seeking to establish her identity, she told them how she had gone on to the secondary school (now closed) and had sung at the concerts. They spoke of other girls who had married, and of their families. They reminisced about the orphanage children and mentioned how well-behaved they had been – 'just like little Protestants' – but they didn't seem interested in Clare. Perhaps, from experience, they sensed that she was one of those for whom things had gone wrong.

She was particularly anxious to see the orphanage photograph album. When she pointed to a photograph of herself they denied that it was her, until she forced them to take it out and read her name on the back. They seemed to be denying the fact of her very existence.

We asked whether we could look inside the orphanage, but they laughed and said, 'What would you want to go into that cold, old place for? It's all empty and locked up.' When we went out, we looked in through the key-hole of the door. All we could see was the flight of stairs which she and so many others had scrubbed till their fingers were raw. Then we walked up the steps to the field, Ballykinlar. All the property had been put up for sale.

On the drive back to Dublin Clare sat chain-smoking, silent and withdrawn. The next day she took the boat for England. We did not hear from her again.

This book has been centred around one orphanage. It has been a human story, recounting the childhood and adult experiences of a group of women over a period of fifty years. With regard to the lovelessness, the brutality, the absence of normal emotional development and destruction of self-esteem which they suffered as children, perhaps there is nothing new in the knowledge of what these do to people, whether inside an institution or a family. But their story has political implications as well. Starting with the inquiry into the fire in 1943 where many of the most important questions were left unanswered, and continuing with the pusillanimity and untruths of the annual reports, and the moral evasions of the investigations into the industrial school system, it is an account of the collusion between state and church, the one turning a blind eye to, or abetting, the other's law-breaking and inhumanity.

Where the church had control, as in the case of 'voluntary' laundry reformatories with their 'morally delinquent' inmates, there was no possibility of interference. Where these areas were inter-twined, as in the case of the industrial schools, the combination was too overwhelming for anyone to challenge. No government minister, no politician or public figure, no departmental administrator or inspector would consider expressing officially any doubts they might have had about the treatment of children in care.

One can imagine the inspectors' visits: the conducted tour of the clean, well-polished rooms and the dormitories with the counterpanes on the beds for their annual airing, the orderly rows of girls in their Sunday best, eating 'the one good dinner we got apart from Christmas'. If they suspected that the reality was different, then what were they to do? Where was the money to come from to make improvements? Who else would look after the children with so little financial reward? Who was going to criticise the nuns when it was generally agreed that they were doing their best? And who else would do the job? Any demand for real change would have required a revolution in the status quo at its most fundamental level. In the event, when things did begin to change, it was the church and not the state which was the initiator and the innovator.

Mental and physical cruelty towards children, whether or not in institutional care, are not the exclusive prerogative of the Catholic Church or of Irish people: nor is bureaucratic irresponsibility. Few countries or institutions wielding excessive or inadequately controlled power have nothing to hide. If this book has any message, it is the old one of the dangers inherent in any situation where a person or group of persons, be they the government, the police, the army, trade unions, a political party or a religious organisation, is permitted to operate outside and unanswerable to the law.

Many of the nuns in our story were cruel to the children in their care. But then their motives for entering the convent may well have been those which would render them least suitable for the care of children. It may have been social, financial or parental pressure – there was enormous social cachet in Ireland in having a daughter a nun – or it may have been because they were unable to cope with the problems of ordinary life. They may have had an idealised view of a nun's existence in an enclosed Order: quiet contemplation, intense spirituality, denial of the gross needs of the flesh. If they then found that they lacked a true vocation, it needed considerable courage to face, as a 'spoiled' nun, the opprobium of parents and society. As their youth passed into maturity and middle age, their days spent in the repetitive rigorous discipline of their religious duties and enduring the petty jealousies and irritations that can exist in a closed-in community, their accumulated frustration and hidden resentment could, only too easily, be vented on the children in their care.

They were faced with the formidable task of being responsible for up to eighty children, a task surely beyond the capacity of the most motherly woman trained in child care. They had to take, as Tina put it, 'what the world threw in at them'. Add to this the general acceptance of the use of violence upon children and a situation could exist where their consciences may not have been perturbed by their actions. As for the kind nuns, or those who stood by, turning their eyes from what they saw happening about them, what could they do? They were caught up within the web of the system, bound by vows of unquestioning obedience.

The general public, too, were silent. Yet too many thousands of children passed through the industrial school system and out into the small, tightly-knit Irish community for the members of that community to have been unaware of how they were treated. The legacy of that treatment is with us today.

Those who asked us not to write this book did so in the belief that the situation is better now. The revelations about the Kincora Boys

Home and the Williamson House Children's Home in Belfast must prove them wrong. Here again was the familiar story of inspectors failing in their duties and of crimes committed against children which would never have been allowed to happen if the regulations had been enforced. Children in care are especially vulnerable. We owe it to them to be eternally vigilant on their behalf.

In August 1985 we returned to Cullies cemetery. On the orphans' grave, which had been changed since our previous visit, lay a faded wreath. A new headstone was in place. All mention of St Josephs and of the orphans had been removed. The inscription reads: 'In loving memory of the Little Ones of St Clare. R.I.P. Children pray for us.'

Notes

Prologue

1. When Dr McQuaid, the Roman Catholic Archbishop of Dublin, returned from Pope John's Vatican Council in 1963 he made a public statement assuring the faithful they had nothing to fear. In Ireland, he said, nothing would change.
2. Examples of this work are to be seen in Dublin's National Museum.
3. Section 44 of the 1908 Act states: 'The expression "Industrial School" means a school for the industrial training of children, in which children are lodged, clothed and fed as well as taught. The expression "Reformatory School" means a school for the industrial training of youthful offenders, in which youthful offenders are lodged, clothed and fed as well as taught.'

Part One

1. This chapter is based on newspaper accounts of the fire and its aftermath, and on conversations and interviews with witnesses.
2. One of the solicitors representing the parents told the authors that the parents might have thought they could get compensation. However, he doubted they would have been able to obtain this because the children were in an industrial school at state expense. One of the nuns we spoke to referred to this indignantly: 'Just imagine trying to sue us. And after we had taken in their children.'
3. On this bunch there was, she said, also one to the dormitory lavatories. It was never explained why these or any of the other internal doors were locked.
4. This latter statement was made in newspapers.
5. When the authors asked two women who had been in the orphanage up to a short time before the fire whether they had ever done fire drill neither of them had any recollection of it. As for pigeon chasing, they did not remember it, nor did they think it possible.
6. An ex-pupil of the 1930s told the authors that the doors were locked in her day, while one survivor of the fire said that they were not.

Part Two

1. A grant of 15*s*. per week for each child was provided by the Department of Education in 1943. Accounts for the orphanage and for the convent were not kept separately, nor did the Department audit them, so that it is impossible to establish how much the children were subsidised over the years by the Order's own funds, as we were informed they were by members of the Order, including the present Mother General.

   The wife of a man who was then under-gamekeeper on Lord Farnham's estate outside Cavan town told us how she had managed to feed and clothe her husband, herself and three children on a wage of £1 a week. On their tiny plot they grew vegetables and kept hens. 'I gave them an egg for breakfast with bread and butter and porridge. Dinner was a rasher and potatoes and cabbage. Tea was soda-bread, butter and jam. I bought a pound of steak for Sunday.'

2. In spite of contributory and non-contributory pensions being introduced in 1935, when she did get it it was through a political favour in the late 1940s. It was then 6*s*. a week.
3. The Act permitted children to be taken out under licence before the age of sixteen to live with respectable persons or to take up an apprenticeship. The manager could issue the licence but had to inform the schools' inspector.
4. Before the fire, St Joseph's was certified for up to 120 children. In 1941 the Annual Report of the Department of Education gave a figure of seventy-six in detention there. After the fire losses the numbers gradually increased again until they peaked at eighty-six in 1954 and thereafter declined.
5. In the Kennedy Report on industrial schools and reformatories published in 1970 it states: 'There is a Diploma Course in Child Care. . . but for some years now not enough applications have been received to enable the course to be held.' Accompanying statistics showed that the majority of those working in the institutions had not received training.
6. When Connie finally managed to get a copy of her birth certificate, it showed a different date of birth from the one she had been given by the nuns.
7. We had suggested this to other girls. Elizabeth Bright's reaction was typical: 'But the nuns had very little to do. We did the cooking and the cleaning and we fed the babies. The only thing Mother Anne did was to make sure we were spic and span and she made us beautiful clothes.'
8. She wet her bed until she was twelve, when she was sent to Dublin for an eye operation. 'Everybody was so kind to me in the hospital that I stopped being afraid and I never wet my bed again.'
9. Tina Martin said this started because Mother Andrew made them clean out the drains. 'They'd be full of slimy things but then someone found a penny and so we all wanted to do it.'
10. Until 1968 secondary education was not compulsory and was mostly fee-paying.
11. School absenteeism was an offence for which children could be committed to industrial schools.
12. A local woman whom we met remembered her mother worrying about her coming home at night 'because of the soldiers from the barracks who used to hang around the convent at night waiting in case the girls got out.'
13. Ally is a voluntary agency set up to place unmarried mothers in people's homes until their babies are born.

Part Three

1. For further information about this institution see *Nothing To Say* by Mannix Flynn (Dublin, Ward River Press, 1983).
2. The last industrial school for the reception of Protestant children shut in 1917. However, voluntary Protestant Children's Homes remained.
3. On finances they made specific recommendations for improving the arrangements by the local authorities of their share of the per capita grant, these authorities apparently often failing to make their proper contribution or being tardy in doing so, thus causing the schools to run up bank overdrafts on which they had to pay interest. The 5*s.* per head granted by the state at the incipience of the official Industrial School system in 1868 was still the same basic rate – although an additional 2*s.*6*d.* per head cost-of-living increase had been given in 1919. Local authorities were paying an average of 4*s.*10*d.* per child. They did not recommend an increase in the basic rate – most costs dropped in the 1930s – but wanted salaries of qualified teachers to be borne by the state rather than to come out of the grant money and that there should be periodic increases to meet rises in the cost of living.

   An interesting point that emerged was that the mothers of illegitimate children, as well as other parents, were, where possible, ordered by the courts at the Committal proceedings to contribute to their children's upkeep. Theoretically, though not in practice, this rule is still in operation. In the early 1960s it was still in effect because a later report (Tuarim) quoted a figure of £9,960 raised from this source.
4. In 1929 the Department of Education noted that the mortality rate in the schools was higher than that of the population as a whole. In that year, out of a total of 6,515 children, 17 died. In 1934, out of a total of 6,420, 25 children died.
5. In 1965 there were 3,419 children in industrial schools. The state paid 35*s.* per week per child and, in a haphazard fashion, the local authorities paid 32*s.*6*d.* per week for maintenance.
6. We heard of two cases where this happened in certified schools from the official in the Department of Education who had acted as intermediary between Elizabeth Bright and her mother.
7. Part of their research was into case histories of Irish boys then in English Borstals. They found that, of 124 boys born in Ireland, 23 had spent some of their childhood in industrial schools in the Republic.
8. This is not born out by figures from the Department of Education. In the period 1959-69 – with one exception – all girls discharged from reformatories went into domestic employment.
9. It took the British police a year to establish his identity. They did this by tracing the unburned corner of a postcard in his pocket addressed to his friend, the late Dr Owen Sheehy-Skeffington.
10. For example, they recommended that the age of criminal responsibility be

raised from eight to twelve. At the time of writing (1984) this has not been done.

11. During the committee's sittings the weekly grants for the children were doubled from £4 2*s*. to £8 5*s*.
12. In an appendix, figures were given showing that of 41 full-time staff in child care, of whom 21 were religious and 20 lay, at a time when there were 2,247 from under a year old up to sixteen in the Industrial Schools, only four had taken child care courses, run by the British Home Office. There were other staff in the institutions – each had its own supervisor and there were teachers, domestic staff and so on.

    They found that 'in almost every case the same staff members are required to perform the duties of teaching, supervision and residential care which means that they are on duty, to all intents and purposes twenty-four hours a day, seven days a week. . . there appears to be a tendency to staff the schools, in part at least, with those who are no longer required in other work. . .'
13. The Committee stated that the principal form of unacceptable social behaviour which had led to admission to these non-certified institutions had been their involvement in prostitution. However, a Sister working in the Gloucester Street convent told us that the majority there had been unmarried mothers. See Chapter 9.
14. The sample was found to highlight a number of factors. 'The first is the generally depressed scores obtained by children in Industrial Schools, indicating that 11.9 per cent are mentally handicapped compared with approximately 2.4 per cent in the population, and that 36.6 per cent are borderline mentally handicapped compared with approximately 12 per cent in the population in general. . . the extent of backwardness (50.3 per cent) on the perceptual abilities tested. . . must be viewed against the figure of 15 per cent in the School Studies from which our norms are derived. . . That these are largely independent of verbal ability indicates the poor development of observation and clear thinking in Industrial and Reformatory Schools.'
15. The Sisters of Mercy, the Sisters of Charity and the Good Shepherds as well as her Order opened these homes, she said.
16. The Tuarim Report makes a similar comment.
17. She said they had a small half-way house hostel where the girls stayed when starting to work outside. They received money from the Departments for the younger girls, 'but the laundry covers the cost of the rest. We get the princely sum of £2 a week for sixty-seven of the others assessed as unemployable.'
18. This was not entirely true. The report identified certain inadequacies which highlighted the need for change.
19. This Act gave the Department of Health the power to admit children into residential and foster homes. It ran parallel to the 1908 Children's Act administered by the Department of Education. Cavan, incidentally,

had one of the highest rates of fostered-out children in Ireland.

20. We experienced the same kind of courteous help in the Department of Local Government. They spent days searching their archives in order to locate the transcripts of the Tribunal of Inquiry into the fire, and we were then given the freedom of their library to examine them at leisure.
21. The new name for reformatory schools.
22. Children under the age of twelve who had committed offences were sent to industrial schools along with the others. Even though these were usually petty offences caused by deprivation, all the children were associated in the public mind with criminal behaviour.